E**r**

CW01082111

English Vocabulary: The Basics offers a clear, non-jargonistic introduction to English vocabulary, the way linguists classify and explain it, and the place of vocabulary in our overall picture of the language, and in society. Introducing a range of terminology for discussing vocabulary, the reader is provided with a coherent, structured description of what we know about words and their meanings.

Key features of this book include:

- Analysis of historical roots of present-day words
- Coverage of the differences between speech and writing and between formality and informality
- Understanding of the social implications of choices that readers make to use standard or non-standard (e.g., regional/dialect) vocabulary
- A focus on British English with reference to a wide range of varieties of English that include North American English, Irish English, Indian English, Malaysian English, Nigerian English and Caribbean English.

Featuring a glossary of key terms, cartoons and illustrations, further reading, reflection points, interesting "factoids" and examples from corpora from around the world, this book is an engaging and thought-provoking read for anyone with an interest in English vocabulary.

Michael McCarthy is Emeritus Professor of Applied Linguistics, University of Nottingham, and Adjunct Professor of Applied Linguistics, University of Limerick. He has (co-)authored and edited 58 books and was co-founder (with Ronald Carter) of the CANCODE spoken English corpus. He has lectured in 46 countries and has been involved in language teaching and applied linguistics for 57 years.

The Basics

The Basics is a highly successful series of accessible guidebooks which provide an overview of the fundamental principles of a subject area in a jargon-free and undaunting format.

Intended for students approaching a subject for the first time, the books both introduce the essentials of a subject and provide an ideal springboard for further study. With over 50 titles spanning subjects from artificial intelligence (AI) to women's studies, *The Basics* are an ideal starting point for students seeking to understand a subject area.

Each text comes with recommendations for further study and gradually introduces the complexities and nuances within a subject.

SUSTAINABILITY (SECOND EDITION)
PETER JACQUES

TRANSLATION
JULIANE HOUSE

TRANSNATIONAL LITERATURE
PAUL JAY

TOWN PLANNING
TONY HALL

WOMEN'S STUDIES (SECOND EDITION)
BONNIE G. SMITH

WORLD PREHISTORY
BRIAN M. FAGAN AND NADIA DURRANI

INFORMATION SCIENCE
JUDITH PINTAR AND DAVID HOPPING

For more information about this series, please visit: www.routledge.com/The-Basics/book-series/B

ENGLISH VOCABULARY

THE BASICS

Michael McCarthy

Routledge
Taylor & Francis Group

LONDON AND NEW YORK

Cover image: Getty Images |CactuSoup

First published 2023
by Routledge
4 Park Square, Milton Park, Abingdon, Oxon OX14 4RN

and by Routledge
605 Third Avenue, New York, NY 10158

Routledge is an imprint of the Taylor & Francis Group, an informa business

British Library Cataloguing-in-Publication Data
A catalogue record for this book is available from the British Library

Library of Congress Cataloging-in-Publication Data
Names: McCarthy, Michael, 1947– author.
Title: English vocabulary: the basics / Michael McCarthy.
Description: Abingdon, Oxon; New York, NY: Routledge, 2023. |
Series: The basics |
Includes bibliographical references and index. |
Summary: "English Vocabulary: The Basics offers a clear, non-jargonistic introduction to
English vocabulary, the way linguists classify and explain it, and the place of vocabulary
in our overall picture of the language, and in society. Introducing a range of terminology
for discussing vocabulary, the reader is provided with a coherent, structured description
of what we know about words and their meanings"—Provided by publisher.
Identifiers: LCCN 2022025666 (print) | LCCN 2022025667 (ebook) |
ISBN 9781032256962 (hardback) | ISBN 9781032256979 (paperback) |
ISBN 9781003284611 (ebook)
Subjects: LCSH: Vocabulary.
Classification: LCC PE1449 .M276 2023 (print) |
LCC PE1449 (ebook) | DDC 428.1—dc23/eng/20220602
LC record available at https://lccn.loc.gov/2022025666
LC ebook record available at https://lccn.loc.gov/2022025667

ISBN: 978-1-032-25696-2 (hbk)
ISBN: 978-1-032-25697-9 (pbk)
ISBN: 978-1-003-28461-1 (ebk)

DOI: 10.4324/9781003284611

Typeset in Bembo
by codeMantra

To the memory of John Sinclair, erstwhile colleague and mentor

CONTENTS

4   Beating about the Bush: Figurative Meaning   78

5   Bear This in Mind: The Mental Lexicon   106

ACKNOWLEDGEMENTS

One Stop Nature Shop, Burnham Deepdale, Norfolk, UK, for permission to reproduce the advertising sign on page 138

Jake Tebbit for permission to reproduce the cartoons on pp. 7, 61, 90, 111, 116, 148 and 155.

INTRODUCTION TO THE READER

Of all the elements that go to make up our language, vocabulary is the biggest. Grammar can seem complex, with its standards and conventions that look like strict laws which we must obey. English pronunciation, often mismatched with the spelling of English words, is also a challenge. But grammar has a limited set of structures to play with, and standard English pronunciation uses a limited set of vowel and consonant sounds. Vocabulary, in comparison, seems vast and unmanageable, shifting like quicksand, forever throwing out old words and letting in new ones. When we add up all the individual words, all the word combinations, and all the meanings and nuances, we find hundreds of thousands of words and expressions. What is more, English vocabulary long ago broke the umbilical cord that tied it to England. English is a world language, used across the globe. That makes its vocabulary all the richer.

English vocabulary is a huge subject to cram into a short, introductory book. However, in just six chapters, I hope to give you a flavour of the fascinating complexity of the world of words. How are words formed? Where did all those words come from? What do they mean, literally and figuratively? How do we acquire and store thousands of them in our minds, ready for use? What roles do they play in our social worlds? These are some of the questions we explore in this book. I've tried to present the basics in an accessible way without over-simplifying things. If the book sparks your interest in vocabulary, there is more than enough further reading you can do to keep you busy for years.

DOI: 10.4324/9781003284611-1

A WORD OR TWO ABOUT WORDS

WHAT DO WE MEAN BY 'VOCABULARY'?

For most people, vocabulary means words, and that is a useful starting point for this book. However, in the study of language, things are rarely as simple as they look, and we need to dig deeper into the terms we use to understand how things work. In fact, the word **vocabulary** can refer to a number of different, but connected, things. It can refer to all the words in a language, so we can say that 'the present-day vocabulary of English' has been influenced over the centuries by Latin, French, etc. (which we will look at in greater detail in Chapter 2). We can also say that someone *has* a large or very learned vocabulary, meaning all the words a person has at their command, either to understand or use or both, and we will take that theme up later too. And we often comment about a little toddler and how much vocabulary they have *acquired* and how quickly, which is another theme we will come back to later in the book. We also talk about a writer's range of words found in their work and which we associate with their unique style, so we might talk about Shakespeare's vocabulary, or of 'poetic' vocabulary, which we touch upon in Chapters 2 and 6. Sometimes we talk about the vocabulary of law, or of science and technology, in which case we are referring to specific sets of terminology used by people involved in those professions. If you are learning a foreign language, you might be given a vocabulary test now and then, and you can be sure it would focus on words and their meanings rather than correct grammar or your skill in composing an essay. And if you were an English speaker and saw a book entitled *A French Vocabulary*, you

DOI: 10.4324/9781003284611-2

would expect to find lists of French words and explanations and/or translations of them into English.

THE 'ENGLISH' IN ENGLISH VOCABULARY

We come up against further complications the moment we talk about *English* vocabulary. English vocabulary can mean many different things. In this book, it will mostly refer to all the words in use in countries where English is a main or official language, though, because I am British, most of the examples will be from British English. The examples are not chosen because I think British vocabulary is in any way superior to, say, North American, Australian, Indian, or Caribbean English vocabulary; it is not. No language or variety of a language is superior to any other. The British examples will be used to illustrate the way vocabulary works in a great many varieties of English, and in other languages for that matter, and occasionally we will consider examples from other languages to help us better understand how English works and how vocabulary works in general.

A study of English vocabulary could mean a focus on the verbal repertoire of just the inhabitants of England and an examination of its long history over 2,000 years. But even when we look back to the distant past, as we shall do in Chapter 2, to the Anglo-Saxon era of 1,500 years ago, it is difficult to delineate one overall label for 'Old English' owing to the existence of various dialects, as the scholar Richard Hogg points out (Hogg 2006). Terms such as *Old English* and *Modern English*, and contemporary labels such as *Yorkshire English* or *Cockney* are useful shorthand, but we should never forget the complexity of the phenomena they are labelling.

English vocabulary can also refer to all the words in use in any country where English is the first or main language, such as the USA, Canada, Ireland, and New Zealand. But English has spread globally, to become a language used in daily life in countries as far apart as Guyana, Nigeria, India, Malaysia, and Fiji, so 'English vocabulary' might well include how English words are used in those countries as well as how words and ways of speaking from local, indigenous languages are used side-by-side to create 'new Englishes'. Finally, there is English as a language of international communication, often used as a *lingua franca*, that is to say, between people for whom English is not a native or first language. The picture is quite complex, and this 'basics' book cannot do it complete justice.

INFORMATION ADD-ON

More than 50 countries have English as one of their official languages. They include countries as widely geographically dispersed as Bangladesh, Myanmar, Sudan, Sierra Leone, Cyprus, Malta, The Bahamas, Vanuatu, Barbados, Namibia, and Qatar. Not everyone in those countries can speak English fluently, and not everyone uses English on a daily basis, but English is very visible in public life and in the media. Most of the countries have English as a result of their history as part of the British Empire. These different varieties of English have developed their own vocabularies alongside the original colonizing variety of English.

AT LEAST WE KNOW WHAT WORDS ARE ... DON'T WE?

SPACED OUT

We said above that thinking of vocabulary as words was a good starting point for this book, but this raises further tricky questions. The most obvious one is: what is a word? The simplest answer is 'the characters between spaces in a written text'.

This sentence has five words.

We can say it has five words because we can see the spaces separating them. However, when we speak at normal speed in friendly conversation, we may only take a breath now and then, and everything just merges into a stream of sound with no 'spaces'. That is why, when you hear people speaking a new language for the first time which you have never heard before, it is almost impossible to make out where one word ends and another word begins. A famous railway station sign in North Wales reads:

*LLANFAIRPWLLGWYNGYLLGOGERYCHWYRND-
ROBWLLLLANTYSILIOGOGOGOCH*

If you have no knowledge of the Welsh language, you could easily think it was one word, and, in a sense, it is, since there are no spaces, and it is the name of one single village. However, anyone who knows Welsh can see many different individual Welsh words inside the long string of characters (words which mean *church, Mary, hazel, pool, white, red*, etc.) and which give the name its usual English translation of 'The church of Saint Mary in the hollow of white hazel trees near the rapid whirlpool by Tysilio's church of the red cave'. Spaces, or the absence of them, are not a completely reliable clue to where one word ends and another begins.

EYES AND EARS

We all feel we know a large number of words of our language and that we can instantly recognize when we see or hear something that is not likely to be a word in our language. If I write *zmoeoglij*, you will probably react by saying it's not an English word. You might say it's not English because, although you have a large and learned vocabulary, you've never come across it before, or because you've looked it up and it doesn't appear in any English dictionary. But you might also reject it because it seems to break the rules or conventions of how English words are formed. You might observe that the letters *zm* can come in the middle of a word (e.g., *gizmo, quizmaster*), but not at the beginning of a word, that there's a weird combination of vowels in the middle (*oeo*), and that English words don't end in *ij*, and that it's not at all clear if it's a noun, or verb, or what, and you would be right on all counts. You might also feel you can't see anything in it which *means* anything. The linguist David Singleton makes the point that sound, spelling, grammar, and meaning all play a part in how we recognize words (Singleton 2016: chapter 1). So, in one sense, words are what speakers of any given language accept as meaningful units of sound or writing which follow the grammatical, spelling, and pronunciation conventions of that language.

IT JUST FEELS RIGHT

We have a general feel, born of our lifetime of experience, for what letters and what sounds can be put together to form English words.

Lewis Carroll, the nineteenth-century author of the children's stories *Alice in Wonderland* and *Through the Looking-Glass, and What Alice Found There* (Carroll, 1872/1998), was able to exploit this kind of knowledge that English speakers have in his famous poem about a hero doing battle with a monster, *The Jabberwocky*. Many of the important words in the poem are invented, nonsense words. The hero's sword is described as *vorpal*, the monster is called a *manxome* foe, and the dark forest where the battle takes place is described as *tulgey*. All of these words were made up by Lewis Carroll but we feel instinctively that they sound possible; they are composed of bits we are familiar with from other words, and they create images in our minds – associations with monsters, dark forests, and heroic struggles – they *mean* something (Figure 1.1).

Lewis Carroll's invented words could hardly be said to be part of most people's vocabulary, despite their curiously familiar shapes and sounds.

INFORMATION ADD-ON

The *Oxford English Dictionary* (OED) has included some of Lewis Carroll's invented words, including *vorpal*, which it defines as 'keen, deadly'; it also notes that the poet W. H. Auden used it in 1941. The OED also includes entries for *manxome*, *uffish*, *tulgey*, and *burble*. *Tulgey* has been used by other writers since Carroll invented it, so he had obviously captured something basic about the formation of English vocabulary – his invented words *feel* right.

I SEE WHAT YOU MEAN

MORPHEMES

Our feeling that there is meaning in Lewis Carroll's nonsense words leads us to a more reliable definition of a word, since a word must consist of at least one bit that means something. This one essential bit is called a **morpheme**. *Car, box, park, photo, leather, sycamore,* and *tomato* each consist of one morpheme, even though they may consist of more than one syllable: *pho-to, lea-ther, sy-ca-more,* and

Figure 1.1 The Jabberwock.
Source: © Jake Tebbit 2022.

to-ma-to all have more than one syllable. A **syllable** is a vowel sound and any consonants attached to it.

Many words consist of more than one morpheme, so in the word *composer,* we see three syllables (*com-pos-er*), with one morpheme which expresses the action of 'composing' or creating something, and a morpheme *-er* indicating that we are referring to a person or thing which does that action, which we are familiar with from other words such as *writer, teacher, painter, printer, marker,* and *screwdriver.*

For most people, *composer* expresses two ideas: 'compose' and 'person'. Anyone with a knowledge of Latin or medieval French might also break the meaning of *compose* down a little further, with *com* (together) and *poser* (put) giving us the present-day meaning of 'put together/create'. However, for most English speakers, the ancient origins of words may be completely invisible in present-day words. That does not mean that the origins of words are irrelevant. In fact, we can only fully understand the richness of English vocabulary by looking at where it has all come from, which we shall do in the next chapter.

REFLECTION POINT

Look at these English words and ask yourself how many different morphemes you can see in them. Your answers may be different from other people's, depending on your knowledge of ancient classical languages or modern European languages. A good dictionary will tell you the origins of these words and how they are composed.

Subterranean   ombudsman   aristocratic   machismo   photographic

TAKING WORDS TO PIECES

Consider these sentences and what the words in bold have in common:

> She **posed** for me while I painted her portrait.
> This is the best **position** for the noticeboard.
> That's an interesting **proposal**.
> The rebels **deposed** the government during the civil war.

We have *posed, position, proposal,* and *deposed.* In the last three, we can see an echo of the idea of pose in the first sentence. We can say that *pose* (or *pos*) is a **root** to which we can attach morphemes before or after. In this case, we have *pro-* and *de-* attached before the root (*proposal* and *deposed*); these are **prefixes**. In *proposal* and *position*, we can see morphemes attached after the root: *-al* and *-ition*. These are **suffixes**. The process of adding prefixes and suffixes is called **derivation**; the words we end up with are called derived words. Derivation is one of the most important ways in which new English words are created. Other examples of derived words are the root *form* giving us *reform, deform* as well as *formation, formative,* and *reformer; act* gives us *react, enact, active, activate, deactivate,* and *action.* Suffixes often change words from one word class to another: a verb can become an adjective (*act > active*) or a noun (*act > action*), and the meaning can be changed by adding prefixes (*rewrite* = write again, *impossible* = not possible).

Some prefixes and suffixes are used more often than others in the creation of derived words: they are more **productive**. For example, the suffix *-dom* in nouns such as *freedom, kingdom,* and *boredom* is not very productive and nouns ending in *-dom* are far fewer than nouns ending in *-ity* (*activity, security, ability,* etc.).

CORPUS EVIDENCE

A search for nouns ending in different suffixes in the British National Corpus (BNC) 1994 shows just how much more productive some suffixes are compared to others. The graph shows how many different nouns there are in the corpus ending in each suffix (Figure 1.2).

Examples: *sensation, conformity, childhood,* and *boredom.*

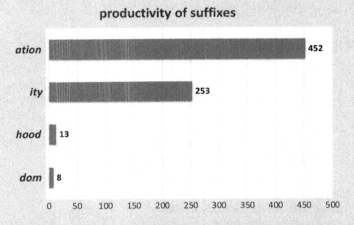

Figure 1.2 Productivity of suffixes in the BNC 1994.

GRAMMAR AND LEXIS

In *posed* and *deposed* in the examples above, we have *-ed* after the root. This morpheme shows us the tense – that the action took place in the past – it is an element of English grammar. It is an **inflection**, which is an example of a **grammatical morpheme**. Other examples of inflections are *we write > she writes > I was writing > they have written; a tree > five trees; one bus > two buses.*

Grammatical morphemes express grammatical meanings such as tense (present/past), and number (singular/plural). Some grammatical morphemes are freestanding words, i.e., they are written with spaces before and after. These include personal pronouns (e.g., *you, she, they*), prepositions (e.g., *at. of, in, to*), and conjunctions (e.g., *and, but, or*). These words are called **grammar words** or **function words**. We will not give much attention to them in this book because we are dealing with **lexis** (another word for vocabulary, in contrast to grammar). **Lexical words** are words that have content – words which 'word the world', the nouns, verbs, adjectives, and adverbs we use to describe our universe and to express our experiences.

WORDS STICK TOGETHER

COMPOUNDS

A word must consist of at least one morpheme, a piece of language that means something to that language's speakers. Many words, as we have seen, have more than one morpheme, but words also club together to create meanings which may or may not be separated by spaces in writing. Consider these combinations of morphemes. In most cases, the spaces are optional – some people write them as one word or use a hyphen; some write them with spaces:

sea shore/seashore
waste-paper basket/wastepaper basket
smart phone/smartphone

Each of these, whether written with a hyphen, with spaces, or without spaces, expresses one single idea or thing. *Sea shore, seashore,* and *coast* all express places where the land meets the sea, *wastepaper basket* and *bin* are things into which we discard stuff, and *smartphone* and *tablet* are types of portable electronic devices. Whether as one word or two or three words together, with or without hyphens, the examples express single ideas. *Seashore, wastepaper basket,* and *smartphone* are **compounds**: individual words have come together to form 'big words' that express single meanings. If we see a sign saying *BUS STOP*, we immediately process it to mean a place where you can get on or off a bus; we don't usually spend time pondering whether it is a local campaign to stop buses entering the neighbourhood, or a barrier to prevent buses entering an area, or a place where buses always break down.

In many cases, everyone agrees on where spaces should be written and where not. English speakers do not normally write *weekend* as *week-end*, or *timetable* as *time table* or *time-table*, even though we can see different morphemes and even though they were once upon a time written with hyphens or spaces. One reviewer of a book on hyphenation in 1951 already at that time was able to refer to hyphenated forms such as *guest-room, hub-bub,* and *look-out* (normally written as single words) as 'fossils of the Hyphen Age' (Summey 1951: 479). On the other hand, few would ever write *washingmachine* for *washing machine* or *windscreenwipers* for *windscreen wipers*.

Christina Sanchez-Stockhammer, in her book on the spelling of English compounds, says that compounds 'usually start off their life with the constituents separated by a space (girl friend), then go through a hyphenated stage (girl-friend) and finally finish as a solid, uninterrupted sequence of letters (girlfriend)' (Sanchez-Stockhammer 2018: 3). In July 2021, someone posted on a social media group dedicated to discussions about words the question, 'Why is *bedroom* one word but *living room* is two words?'; the correct answer to the question is because that's how people usually write them. There is inconsistency in the use of spaces which may be entirely arbitrary. However, most dictionaries agree on how compounds should be written, and corpora of written texts can also help us resolve doubtful cases by showing us how people usually write them.

CORPUS EVIDENCE

The LADEC project (*Large Database of English Compounds*) is a corpus- and database-originated computerized list of 8,000 words which could potentially be combined to form two-word noun compounds, which produced almost 9,000 compounds after various filtering measures. The researchers then tested people's ability to predict the meanings of the compounds, which was affected by how transparent the meanings were (Gagné *et al.* 2019).

So far, we have looked at noun compounds, that is to say where the final word and the compound as a whole function as a noun (e.g., *desktop*, *shoelace*, *dishwasher*, *motorway*). These are extremely common. However, corpora show that there is a range of types made up of different word classes with different functions, albeit some combinations are more productive than others. Bauer and Renouf's (2001) corpus-based study has a wealth of examples of different types. Table 1.1 shows examples of different types, with the usual grammatical function of each word and the usual function of the compound.

Table 1.1, as well as showing us different sorts of combinations, demonstrates how flexible the word classes are in English. Words do not have *a priori* fixed word-class labels; we derive a word's class from how people have used it. Over time, words from one word class can be adapted to function in a different class, called **class conversion**. For example, the American linguist Dwight Bolinger traced the evolution of the word *fun* from its use as a noun (e.g., *it was great fun*) to its now more and more frequent use as an adjective, as in *a fun thing to do*, *the fun part of the course*, etc. (Bolinger 1963).

The last two examples in Table 1.1 are derived from a special type of word combination in English: **phrasal verbs**, verbs which consist of a verb and an adverb particle. Our everyday vocabulary is full of such verbs, for example, *lock down*, *get up*, *go away*, *take off*, *set out*, *wind up*, *come in*, and *catch on*. From these, we get a number of phrasal noun and adjective compounds, of which *lockdown* is an example. Other examples of phrasal nouns and adjectives are *takeoff*,

Table 1.1 Examples of English compound types.

Word 1	Word 2	Compound
sea (noun)	sick (adjective)	seasick (adjective)
freeze (verb)	dry (verb or adjective)	freeze-dry (verb)
low (adjective)	rise (verb)	low-rise (adjective)
European (adjective)	style (noun)	European-style (adjective)
hard (adjective)	edged (adjective)	hard-edged (adjective)
take (verb)	away (adverb particle)	takeaway (adjective or noun)
lock (verb)	down (adverb particle)	lockdown (noun)
key (noun)	board (noun)	keyboard (noun)

downturn/upturn, onset, off-putting, outlying, and *incoming.* Phrasal expressions often exist side-by-side with single words of Latin or French origin. Both Latin and French have influenced English vocabulary over many centuries, as we shall see in Chapter 2, especially in the more formal aspects of language use. The equivalent phrasal form is often used in less formal situations compared with the Latin or French word, for example: *put off, push back* in contrast with *postpone;* likewise, *chill out/relax; go up/increase; cut down, bring down/reduce.* We will return to this theme in Chapter 6. Phrasal verbs have existed in English for many centuries (see Rodríguez-Puente 2019), going right back to the Old English era which we look at in Chapter 2, and they form a significant element of English vocabulary. The *Cambridge International Dictionary of Phrasal Verbs* (CUP 1997) contains over 4,500 phrasal verbs in British, American, and Australian English which were in use at the time of publication.

Some compounds consist of words which come together because of sound patterns. Some consist of two words which vary in their vowel sounds, for example, *tip-top, flip-flop, sing-song, crisscross, chit-chat,* and *riffraff.* These are called **ablaut** compounds. Some are **rhyming** compounds: *hobnob, ragbag, teeny-weeny,* and *fuddy-duddy.* Others are examples of reduplication, the repetition of the same morphemes: *bye bye, weewee,* and *hush-hush.* As we can see, these are sometimes written as two words, sometimes as one (for more examples, see Wang (2005)). These sound-motivated compounds are often colourful, expressive, and playful and include items often used in baby-talk such as *moo-moo* (cow), *bow-wow* (dog), etc.

MULTI-WORD UNITS

So far, we have looked at how words from the major word classes (nouns, verbs, adjectives, adverbs) combine to form compounds. Another type of strong bond between words is created when strings of words are used time and time again, so often that they become routines or fixed formulae for expressing unitary meanings. Everyday examples include *see you later, happy birthday, good morning, thank you very much,* and *how's it going?* These are particularly common in speaking.

If we have a corpus and set up the computer software to analyse how often strings of words are repeated, we soon find that thousands of two-word, three-word, and four-word sequences are repeated hundreds, even thousands of times (depending on how much data we look at). This is such a common feature of any corpus that we have to conclude that not only are there 'big words' in the form of compounds, but there are also many 'big words' that are routine repetitions of two, three, four, or more words and that these **multi-word units** or **chunks** often express single, formulaic meanings, just as compounds do.

Let's consider the most common strings of two, three, four, and five words in the Spoken BNC 2014 corpus. This is a corpus of informal spoken British English published in 2014, consisting of 11.5 million words (Love *et al.* 2017). Table 1.2 gives examples of the top ten most frequent two-word strings and how many times each one occurs in the corpus.

It is important to remember that the computer has no idea what a word is or which multi-word strings count as units for users for any language. The computer just counts letters and spaces and how often sequences of letters and spaces are repeated, so it will also throw in sequences such as *yeah-yeah*, *but you*, or *and I*, which, although very frequent, do not represent meaningful units for native speakers and expert users of the language. However, we do not

Table 1.2 Frequent two-word strings, Spoken BNC 2014.

String	Frequency
you know	45,984
I think	42,815
and then	22,650
I mean	19,450
kind of	11,651
as well	10,165
I thought	7,516
or something	6,815
I dunno	3,955
and stuff	3,706

dismiss strings such as *you know, I mean, kind of, or something, and stuff*, since they fulfil important functions in conversation which we will discuss in Chapter 6.

Frequent multi-word units of three, four, and five words in the Spoken BNC 2014 include the following:

> *a bit of, you know what, a couple, and stuff like that, I can't remember, do you know what I mean, I was gonna say, at the end of the day, don't worry about it, and all the rest of it, and all that kind of stuff, in the middle of the night*

All of these, like the two-word strings, constitute meaningful units that have important functions in everyday conversation, where people interact with one another, tell stories, organize the conversation, etc. My co-author Ronald Carter and I published lists of what we called **clusters** (the same as **chunks** here) consisting of two to five words taken from spoken and written corpora and classified them according to their functions, which included relations of time and place, interpersonal functions, the use of vague language, linking ideas, and organizing turn-taking in conversation (Carter and McCarthy 2006: 828–837).

Multi-word units (chunks) are not extras in our account of the English vocabulary; they are an integral part of it. Research into everyday conversation shows that they form a large part of what we say, perhaps half of all the words we use (Erman and Warren 2000).

INFORMATION ADD-ON

Multi-word units are often just as frequent as everyday single words; sometimes they are more frequent. A random sample of chunks beginning with *in*, compared with a random sample of nouns beginning with *s-*, in both cases with frequencies greater than 1,000 in the written documents of the BNC 1994, shows the extent to which multi-word units form an integral element of the vocabulary (Figure 1.3).

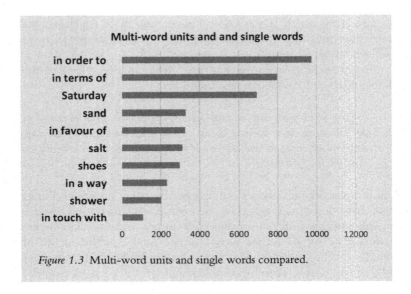

Figure 1.3 Multi-word units and single words compared.

IDIOMS

Some multi-word units are quite **transparent**; we can see what they mean just from the words that make them up, so everyday expressions such *as at the moment, around the corner, a couple of, all the time, without doubt* and so on are not difficult to process. Other multi-word units vary in their degrees of transparency such that many are almost completely **opaque** – you cannot work out what the expression means just from the sum of its parts. These are **idioms**. However, **idiomaticity** is a matter of degree; it is not absolute, and some idioms are more opaque than others. The expression *the right place at the right time* occurs more than 60 times in the British National Corpus of 1994, so it seems to be quite fixed without much scope for variation; at the same time, it is quite transparent. At the other extreme, the expression *on the hoof*, as in 'make a decision on the hoof' (meaning quickly, without time to consider the situation properly) is not at all transparent – you either know what it means or you do not, or it takes a bit of guessing in context as to what it might mean. In between are idioms which are usually decipherable in context. If we see a sentence 'She's been awarded a prize for her poetry; she's over the moon', we can guess that the meaning of *over the moon* is something positive, rather than 'angry' or 'ashamed'. We shall look more closely at this type of meaning in Chapter 4.

COLLOCATION

There is one last way that words combine which we have not mentioned yet. It is a looser sort of combining than compounds, multi-word items, and idioms, yet it is still a significant feature of the vocabulary. Words combine with each other in ways which are more likely or less likely and this relationship is called **collocation**. Some pairings of words are more likely to occur than others. Take for example, colour words. *Red, blue, green* can combine with a huge number of nouns. We would hardly think it unusual to hear about *a blue sky, a blue sweater, a blue pen, a blue book, a blue bag, a blue car, red hair, a red jacket, green grass*, etc. However, the colour *blonde* is much more restricted and is usually only combined with words connected with hair (*hair, tresses, curls, locks*, etc.) or *man/woman, child*. We would not refer to *a blonde car*, or to *a blonde sweater*, or to *a blonde dog*. We could talk about *a beige car* or *a beige sweater*, but not *beige hair*. *Blonde* and *beige* **collocate** differently.

Collocation was first brought to prominence in language study by the British linguist John Rupert Firth, who famously said 'You shall know a word by the company it keeps' (Firth 1951/1957: 11). The more restricted company that a word keeps, the stronger it collocates with its partners. *Blonde*, as we have mentioned, collocates with very few words, so the combinations *blonde hair* and *blonde curls* are **strong collocations** – the 'glue' that binds them is tough and very adhesive. *Good* collocates with potentially thousands of words, e.g., *good morning, good meal, good computer, good car, good weather, good boy, good time, good health*, etc. These are **weak collocations** – the glue that binds them is not very strong at all, and *good* is happy to strike up a relationship with any old word within limits.

In between *good* and *blonde*, there are tens of thousands of other English words. How do we know if they are weak or strong collocators? This is where the computer comes in. By analysing a corpus to see which words are found together, the computer can give a precise statistical count for how likely or unlikely it is that any two words will be found in the same environment.

RECIPES FOR NEW WORDS

WORDS COME AND GO

The vocabulary of English is constantly growing. Hundreds of new words enter the language every year. New words come in and existing words or parts of words are commandeered to cover new meanings brought about by technological or social change. For example, the language of computers and the internet has expanded massively in the last 20 years (*smartphone, tweet, emoji, selfie*, to name but a few). New words may come in and old words may drop out. When I was a child, we used the word *wireless* for what most people now call the radio. Machines and equipment can quickly become obsolete as technology advances.

> **REFLECTION POINT**
>
> How many of these words are you familiar with? They all refer to equipment which was commonly used during the second half of the twentieth century.
>
> radiogram telex camcorder modem pager fax Walkman carphone

Existing, but less frequent, words may become very frequent because of events such as the coronavirus pandemic of 2020 (e.g., *pandemic, quarantine, covid, lockdown, self-isolating*). *Pandemic, quarantine,* and *lockdown* have existed as less commonly used terms for many decades but within weeks they became everyday words on everyone's lips because of the global health crisis of 2020. The word *landline* existed but was not much used outside of technical contexts until mobile phones came along; now *landline* contrasts with *mobile* when talking about phones and phone numbers.

NOTHING NEW UNDER THE SUN

There are several different ways in which new words can enter the language. What may surprise us is that completely new words that have little or no connection with any existing words are rare. Anyone can make up a word, but only if the great majority of people start to use it in a community could it be said to be part of the vocabulary of that community. Most 'new' words consist of new combinations of existing morphemes.

We have already mentioned derivation. Using Greek and Latin roots and adding prefixes and suffixes is particularly common in scientific and technical language. Recent examples include *entheogen, codeathon, tomophobia,* and *aphantasia,* all of which have been incorporated into major dictionaries. Greek and Latin morphemes are so pervasive in existing and new words in English, that two scholars, James Morwood and Mark Warman, have produced a textbook for students just about the influence of Greek and Latin on English words (Morwood and Warman 2008).

INFORMATION ADD-ON

The *OED* published an update for the three months to June 2021 which included nearly 700 new words and new meanings for existing words (see https://public.oed.com/updates/).

New items don't make their way into big, famous dictionaries until the dictionary-writers (**lexicographers**) are satisfied that the items are being widely used. The American *Merriam Webster* dictionary publishes a watchlist, a sort of standby list, of words the lexicographers are monitoring as possible candidates for the dictionary (see https://www.merriam-webster.com/topics/words-were-watching).

HALF AND HALF

Some new words are **blends**. That is, they consist of morphemes from two different words put together to form one new word. Table 1.3 shows some examples of **blending**.

Table 1.3 Examples of blending.

Word 1	Word 2	Blend
smoke	fog	smog
emotion	icon	emoticon
breakfast	lunch	brunch
motor	hotel	motel
documentary	drama	docudrama
stay	vacation	staycation

Sometimes, the forms we find in blends act more like prefixes and suffixes than fused words. Part of the noun *alcoholic* denoting a person addicted to alcohol can be seen acting like a suffix in *workaholic, shopaholic,* and *chocoholic.* Likewise, *agriculture* acts like a prefix in *agribusiness* and *agritourism.* Since the Watergate political scandal in the United States in the 1970s, *-gate* has been applied to other scandals and controversies (*Irangate, Dianagate, Partygate*). The American *Merriam-Webster Dictionary* online devotes a page to *-gate* words referring to scandals.[1]

Staycation (holidaying at home instead of going way) rose to prominence in 2020 when the global health crisis meant people were unable to travel. Blends are creative combinations which grab our attention, they are **salient**, even though they account for only a small number of the new words that regularly enter the English vocabulary. The researcher Isabel Balteiro says of blends: 'it is their striking, innovative and playful nature that makes blends more visible than their sheer numbers or their quite reduced productivity would allow' (Balteiro 2013: 884), and as another scholar points out, blends are often short-lived and die out of the language (Cannon 1986). *Staycation* may die out or become less frequent as people start going away again; only time will tell. We saw how Lewis Carroll invented words for his *Jabberwocky* poem; *slithy* was one of these (the *OED* suggests it is a blend of *slimy* and *lithe*, combining the idea of slime and flexible movement). We also saw that apart from a handful of reuses by well-known writers, Carroll's invented words never caught on.

KEEP IT SHORT

Language is very economical, and if we can say something in a shorter way, we usually do, so some new words and expressions are cut-down forms of longer words. We say *phone* instead of *telephone, exam* instead of *examination, ad* or *advert* instead of *advertisement*, we often say *bye* instead of *goodbye*, all of which usually happen over time as a matter of convenience. Nobody ever says *omnibus* now to refer to a bus, even though *omnibus* was once the full form of the word; we say *the web* rather than *the world-wide web* and refer to *my phone* rather than *my mobile phone*.

Shortening words is called **clipping**. Informal Australian English seems to be particularly prone to clipping, with examples such as *barbie* (barbecue), *footy* (football), *sunnies* (sunglasses), *rellies* (relatives), and *arvo* (afternoon). The linguist Anna Wierzbicka suggests that such clippings often express conviviality and humour or, in the case of shortenings such as *anthro* (anthropologist) and *journo* (journalist), that the speaker is showing their familiarity with the word (Wierzbicka 1986). And this kind of shortening is not just a feature of English; colloquial French has many examples of the phenomenon (e.g., *labo = laboratoire, ado = adolescent, comme d'hab = comme d'habitude, hélico = hélicoptère*).

Another way of shortening words is just to use initials. **Initialism** is particularly common when referring to the names of well-known institutions, e.g., *BBC* = British Broadcasting Corporation, *CNN* = Cable News Network, *CIA* = Central Intelligence Agency, *ABC* = Australian Broadcasting Corporation, *CAF* = Confederation of African Football, *AK* = Athletics Kenya. Sometimes sets of initials are pronounced as words, e.g., *PIN* = personal identification number, *STEM* = science, technology, engineering and mathematics, *NASA* = National Aeronautics and Space Administration. These are examples of **acronyms**.

LENDING AND BORROWING

English has always been rather easy-going when it comes to importing words from other languages, just as it has exported words to other languages. In Chapter 2, we shall see how waves of invaders and conquerors (Romans, Anglo-Saxons, Vikings, and Normans) brought new words from their languages into the existing languages of Britain, and that process of importation has never stopped, albeit many new words came about because of British conquest and colonization of other lands rather than vice-versa. Overseas adventures in trade brought new goods and encounters with new cultures, for example, English incorporated a number of **loanwords** from the Indian subcontinent. In my 2021 book on grammar and style, I said the following:

> We don't have to go far into the alphabet before we find *ashram, avatar, bhaji, bangle, chapatti, chutney, bungalow, catamaran, cummerbund, dekko, dinghy, Diwali,* etc. All of these will be familiar in varying degrees to British and American English speakers and speakers of other varieties of English.
>
> (McCarthy 2021c: 94)

In recent decades, words related to food and drink that have entered British English as a result of Britons becoming more adventurous in matters of cuisine include *pizza, sushi, taco, panini, latte, cappuccino, tikka, kebab,* and *tequila,* borrowed from lands and regions as far apart as Japan, Mexico, India, Pakistan, the Middle East, and Italy.

Some loanwords fill gaps in meaning or describe a social phenomenon for which English had no ready-made terms. When a language does not seem to have a convenient word to express something, we call this a **lexical gap**. *Juggernaut*, with its origin in the Hindu tradition of conveying the effigy of a god on a massive carriage, became a useful term to describe extremely large, heavy lorries in the twentieth century, as well as becoming a metaphor for any unstoppable negative force or institution. *Ombudsman*, from Swedish, referring to an official whose job is to investigate complaints against maladministration by the government and civil servants, became an 'English' word when a similar official role was introduced in the United Kingdom and other English-speaking countries in the mid-twentieth century. Now there are ombudsmen in various domains of public life, such that few people would even be remotely aware that the word came from Swedish.

INFORMATION ADD-ON

Here are some more examples of English words borrowed from other languages.

satsuma (Japanese) junta (Spanish) crayon (French) kayak (Inuit)

wiki (Hawaiian) galore (Gaelic) schadenfreude (German) amok (Malay)

soprano (Italian) sauna (Finnish) boomerang (Aboriginal Australian)

Loanwords are often anglicized in spelling and pronunciation, for example, *galore* comes from the Gaelic *go leór*, meaning a sufficiency or abundance of something. *Sauna*, pronounced /ˈsaʊnə/ in Finnish (as in *pound*), has been anglicized to /ˈsɔːnə/ (as in *law*).

CORPORA: LETTING THE DATA SPEAK

USING A CORPUS

One way of finding out which words should be listed as words in the vocabulary of English is to search a huge, computerized collection of texts known as a **corpus** (plural **corpora**). In this book, I will often make mention of corpora and how we can use them to study vocabulary. In a very large corpus such as the British National Corpus of 1994 (hereafter BNC 1994), we can easily get statistics, using dedicated software, for how many different words there are and how frequent (or rare) they are, so that we can judge whether a word is in common use or whether it is a one-off such as some of Lewis Carroll's *Jabberwocky* words. The BNC 1994 consists of almost 100 million words of text taken from spoken and written sources, so it can give us an accurate and reliable portrait of a wide range of spoken and written British English as it existed during the time the texts were collected, i.e., in the last part of the twentieth century. The corpus was updated with a new spoken version, the Spoken BNC 2014, consisting of 11.5 million words of transcribed conversations recorded in the UK from 2012 onwards.

The BNC does not tell us the whole story of English vocabulary. We also have to look at data from historical sources, which we do in Chapter 2. And we will always need to keep an eye on the vocabulary of the present day as it is constantly changing, with many new words having entered the language even since the relatively short stretch of time since 2014. Then there is the question of data from spoken and written texts in other varieties of English, many of which are well documented, for example, in the International Corpus of English (ICE) and in corpora of English data collected separately in different countries and regions, for example, North America, Ireland, Singapore, and India.

CORPUS EXAMPLE (1): HARD-WORKING WORDS

A general corpus of conversational English such as the Spoken BNC2014 can tell us what words are most commonly used by people in their day-to-day speaking. At the click of a mouse, we can get a frequency list of all the words in the corpus in their different forms. The list of **word forms** will include everything from grammar words (articles, pronouns, prepositions, etc.) to all the various forms any given word can have. This means we may get a different frequency for the word form *said* as opposed to *say* or *saying*, for example, and this could be important, revealing how often people quote one another: *x said*, or *x says*, or *x was saying* may have different functions (see the discussion in McCarthy 1998: ch.8).

A frequency list can tell us not only what words are in circulation but also the extent of the work each word does in the corpus. Figure 1.4 shows us what percentages of all the words in the corpus are accounted for by the top 1,000 most frequent words, then the next 1,000 and the next 1,000, and so on. We can see that the first 1,000 word forms work much harder than all the rest, accounting for 84% of all the words in the corpus. The next most frequent 1,000 words only account for just under 4%, the next 1,000 under 2%, and the next 1,000 just 1%. In other words, the 3,000 most frequent words account for close on 90% of the content of the corpus. Written language has a wider range of words which work harder, but conversation is what most people do most of the time; it is a fundamental way of communicating, and it seems it can be carried out efficiently by 'scaffolding' all the less frequent words (the words with the heaviest lexical content) upon a core of heavy-duty words. Such information could be useful, for example, in choosing priorities in the teaching of English as a second language.

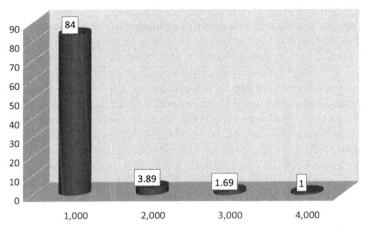

Figure 1.4 Hard-working words

CORPUS EXAMPLE (2): SPEAKING VERSUS WRITING

Speaking and writing share a great deal of vocabulary; we don't have to access a completely different dictionary when we change from one to the other. But how much do they share? A corpus can help us answer that question. My co-researcher Paula Buttery and I compared the written fiction segment (16 million words) of the BNC 1994 with the 1994 spoken segment (10 million words). When there is a slight imbalance in the size of datasets as in this case (16-10), we **normalize** the statistical output: we recompute the total occurrences of individual words as occurrences per 1 million words. Buttery and I found that the 100 most frequent words in each dataset overlapped to about 65%, that is to say, about two-thirds of the top 100 words were common to both the spoken and written texts (Buttery and McCarthy in press). But when we looked further down our word lists, as the words became less frequent, so the overlap decreased, with only just under half (47%) of the top 2,000 words being shared by the spoken and written data.

The top 100 or so words in any corpus of English texts typically consist of grammatical words (articles, pronouns, prepositions, etc.) and, if it is a **raw frequency list**, it will count each form of a word separately; *speak, speaks, speaking, spoke,* and *spoken* will be treated as different words. However, making the best use of a corpus to understand vocabulary often involves doing more than just looking at a word list of every word form that occurs in the corpus. When we look a word up in a dictionary, we expect to find one main form, its **base form**. For example, if it is a noun, the dictionary entry (sometimes called the **headword**) will be in the singular, not an inflected plural: we look up and find STATUE not *statues*. If it is a verb, we will likewise find the base form, not an inflected form: the dictionary entry will be ARRIVE, not *arrives, arrived,* or *arriving,* and so on. The software that corpus analysts use can search for the base form and all inflected forms of a word and bring them together in what is called a **lemma**. A lemma includes the base form and any inflected forms. The base form chosen for the dictionary entry represents the lemma: STATUE represents both *statue* and *statues*.

The top 100 lemmas in the BNC 1994 spoken list contain a number of items that are clearly lexical items rather than grammar items. These include:

> *well, right, know, think, like, mean, thing, good*

On closer inspection of **concordances** (screen displays of key items and their surrounding text), we can see that these words play important roles as **discourse markers**, words, and chunks which help to organize the speaker's talk and the conversation as a whole or to express speakers' stance towards what they are saying, with chunks such as *you know, I think* and *I mean* being extremely frequent. As regards *like*, we can note that its use as a discourse marker outstrips its use as a verb expressing pleasure. This example from the BNC 1994 shows the discourse markers in action:

[speakers are negotiating a convenient meeting time]
<speaker 1> yeah **right well you know** *any time after sort of six, six thirty you should be able to catch me then*

<speaker 2> **okay** *and is there a particular evening that's best for you?*
<speaker 1> erm, no most evenings it doesn't really matter no
<speaker 2> that's fine, **okay,** *smashing.* **Right, well** *as I say I've got your details here so ...*

(BNC 1994 JJC)

Note also the use of *fine* and *smashing*. These express speakers' reactions to what they hear. Along with other high-frequency words such as *good, great, sure, excellent, definitely,* and *absolutely,* they operate as **response tokens** in conversation. Their most frequent uses in formal writing tend to be as conventional adjectives and adverbs (in examples such as *a great amount of money, will definitely last longer,* and so on). In 2002, I published a corpus study of common response tokens in British and American English; Irish English response tokens have also been investigated (see McCarthy 2002, 2003; O'Keeffe and Adolphs 2008).

The corpus throws up interesting differences between speaking and writing in terms of frequencies, but we also have to rethink some of the terminology we need to talk about vocabulary. The conversational extract above illustrates that we need to incorporate functional terms such as *discourse marker* and *response token* into our description of the lexicon. The conventional word classes of noun, verb, adjective, and adverb are not enough and do not adequately capture what the vocabulary is doing.

CORPUS EVIDENCE

These examples are taken from the many thousands of occasions where speakers say *well actually* in the Spoken BNC 2014. The labels 'S0037' etc. designate different individuals starting to speak. It is not only notable that *well* and *actually* occur together, but also that they often occur at the start of a speaker's turn, the classic position for response tokens (Figure 1.5).

"S0037">well actually when we were there were were they not
"S0043">well actually like my dad and my granddad on my mum's
"S0052">well actually if I drive two by the time I've driven for about
"S0058">well actually I've got a quite a nice timetable for her but I'm
"S0060">well actually it's all sold on him being a good looking
"S0093">well actually the two it is a male female leads you know the
"S0136">well actually they're doing this starting this course now for
"S0157">well actually I don't quote me on that</u> <u n="512"
"S0167">well actually what I would do is I would I would buy a
"S0179">well actually it's a poet and you didn't know it it's a bit more
"S0179">well actually tell him that <anon type="name"
"S0179">well actually it wasn't what I was going for</u> <u n="60"

Figure 1.5 Sample concordance lines for *well actually* (Spoken BNC 2014).

SUMMING UP

In this chapter, we began by considering some of the problems inherent in the term *English vocabulary* and in defining *words*. We then moved on to look at how morphemes create meaning in the vocabulary, combining in different ways to form familiar words. We then examined how words combine into larger units of meaning such as compounds, phrasal verbs, and idioms, and how they occur together in collocations. We also exemplified the main mechanisms by which the vocabulary of English acquires new words. Finally, we took a look at what corpora can do to give us a better understanding of vocabulary.

In the next chapter, we ask the question 'Where did it all come from?' and 'How did the vocabulary of English come to look the way it does today?' I hope you will agree, after reading Chapter 2, that the story of English vocabulary is a fascinating one that is not over yet.

FURTHER READING

Bauer, L. 1983. **English Word-Formation.** Cambridge: Cambridge University Press.

This is a comprehensive introduction to the way words are formed in English, covering all the types outlined in this chapter and a lot more. Chapter 7 is indispensable reading; it gives numerous examples of all the different processes in English word-formation.

Jackson, H. and Zé Amvela, E. (2007) *Words, Meaning and Vocabulary: An Introduction to Modern English Lexicology.* **Second edition. London: Continuum.**
This book covers a wide range of themes and topics in the study of vocabulary and takes further the themes in this chapter around how we define words and word formation. Chapter 1 has a useful section on morphemes. Word formation is covered in Chapter 4.

Kastovsky, D. (2006). Vocabulary. In R. Hogg and D. Denison (eds.), *A History of the English Language.* **Cambridge: Cambridge University Press, 199–270.**
The chapter by Dieter Kastovsky in Hogg and Denison's edited book gives a good introduction to the study of vocabulary. It covers morphology and word formation and also has a range of historical information which supplements the discussion in Chapter 2 of this book.

Singleton, D. (2016) *Language and the Lexicon: An Introduction.* **Abingdon, Oxon: Routledge.**
David Singleton's book is a good introduction to the study of vocabulary, including how words are formed, as well as many other themes which we cover in this book. Chapters 1 and 3 offer a detailed follow-up on the themes of this chapter (defining words, morphemes, etc.).

NOTE

1 https://www.merriam-webster.com/words-at-play/gate-suffix-scandal-word-history.

WHERE DO ENGLISH WORDS COME FROM?

THE DIM AND DISTANT PAST

During the period 43–70 AD, the Romans colonized Britain and established their authority. They conquered an island where most of the natives spoke what we now call Brittonic or Celtic languages. Although we tend to think that the British tribes the Romans encountered were all Celtic, the archaeological and genetic history of Britain suggests that the picture was more complex, with tribes from continental Europe already present in some southern coastal areas (Oppenheimer 2006: chapters 7–9).

The Celtic languages survive in present-day form in Welsh, Scots Gaelic, Irish, Gaelic, Manx (Isle of Man), and Cornish. We do not have written records of the Brittonic languages of the earliest times. The Brittonic tribes had little use for writing, and it fell to the Romans to introduce writing into Britain. From Roman writings, we know that oral tradition was important to the people of Britain; community knowledge was passed from generation to generation by word of mouth, so we lack records of what the British vocabulary was like at that time. The language of Britain has changed greatly since the time of the Roman conquest; nonetheless, some words and place names in modern English have a Celtic origin and may have been with us in one form or another for millennia.

DOI: 10.4324/9781003284611-3

INFORMATION ADD-ON

These English words all have a Celtic language origin. Some have specialized meanings, for example, landscape or archaeological features,
while others are used in everyday English.

bard: poet   *brogue*: a type of shoe   *corgi*: breed of dog
clan: group of families with the same name   *coracle*: small, round boat
crag: high, rocky area   *cromlech:* ancient stone monument
gull: coast-dwelling bird
loch/lough: lake   *pet*: animal kept for companionship

The Romans brought Latin with them, and Latin has influenced
the vocabulary of English in different ways, at different times, right
up to the present day, through the introduction of official, legal,
religious, academic, scientific, and technical terms. The Romans
occupied Britain for almost 400 years but were not responsible for
the foundation of what we now call English – that was to come
later. Remnants of their Latin language can be seen in some place
names (e.g., *Britannia*: Britain, *Londinium*: London, *Caledonia*: Scotland), albeit many Latin-influenced place-names date from the
Middle Ages, when Latin once again became prominent as an official language in England (Figure 2.1).

THE BEGINNING OF ENGLISH

ANGLO-SAXONS

The next major wave of invaders and incomers was to have a more
profound influence on the language of Great Britain. Tribes from
northern Europe, known as the Jutes, Angles, and Saxons (from
parts of what are nowadays Denmark, Germany, and the Nether-
lands) colonized the eastern and northern parts of Britain, bringing
with them the Germanic Anglo-Saxon language, which became the
language of England from the fifth to the twelfth century AD, what
we call Old English (OE). This was also when the first manuscripts
in English came into existence, providing us with the first proper
evidence of an English vocabulary.

Figure 2.1 The Celtic landscape. Image © Michael McCarthy 2022.

Old English looks very different from modern-day English. Words were subject to inflections (see Chapter 1), which showed case (for example, whether a word was the subject or object in a sentence) tense, number, and gender. Most of these extra bits on words were later dropped. Although an OE text looks very foreign to a modern English reader who has not studied the language, once we get behind the inflected words to their roots and pronunciation, we can sometimes see or hear the seeds of our modern English vocabulary.

In the Anglo-Saxon kingdoms of England, laws began to be written down. The *Law-code of King Æthelberht of Kent* contains a variety of legal texts and records and is one of the earliest books we know of in English. Æthelberht lived in the seventh century. The law-code of the ninth-century King Alfred the Great is another example. Alongside these, we have literary works such as the epic poem *Beowulf* and other heroic poetry, we also have chronicles, charters, and official documents, and so we have a range of sources for understanding where English vocabulary came from.

Figure 2.2 Runic characters. Image © Michael McCarthy 2022.

Latin did not disappear entirely after the Romans left Britain. Latin was also the language of the Christian church, and when England became a Christian country, Latin took on a new role:

> The importance of the role played by Latin goes back to the introduction of Christianity in England at the end of the sixth century, when the Anglo-Saxons were confronted not only with a new language but also with a new medium: Latin as the language – the written language – of the church.
>
> (Nevalainen and Van Ostade 2006: 270).

Nevalainen and Van Ostade then go on to say, 'Latin became the High language and English, in its many different dialects, the Low language' (ibid. 271). The linguist James Milroy observes that

Anglo-Saxon words connected with the church such as *candel* (candle), *mynster* (monastery), and *reogol* (rule) are borrowings from Latin (Milroy 2007). And Latin will reappear later in our story too.

BEGINNING TO LOOK FAMILIAR: CHRONICLES AND MONSTERS

Old English, like any other language, was not static and changed and developed over the centuries. Some later manuscripts, although they still look strange to us in the stylish handwriting of the scribes, contain words that are closely related to present-day vocabulary. The famous ninth-century *Anglo-Saxon Chronicle*, which lists important historical events, tells of terrorizing raids upon north-eastern England by Vikings from Scandinavia in the year 793. There were several versions of the Chronicle, copied and revised up to the eleventh century. Here is the paragraph for the year 793 from an eleventh-century copy of the Chronicle, transcribed by the scholar Michael Swanton, and then a modern English translation.

> 793 **Her** wæron reðe forebecna **cumene ofer Norðanhymbra land, and** þæt **folc** earmlice bregdon. Þær wæron ormete ligræscas, **and** wæron geseowene **fyrene dracan** on þam lyfte **fleogende**. Þam tacnum **sona fyligde** mycel **hunger**.
>
> (Swanton 1971: 22)

These words in bold in modern translation can be spotted in the OE text (also in bold).

> **Here** were cruel omens **come over** the **land** of **Northumbria, and** miserably terrified the **people (folk)**: there were immense sheets of lightning, **and fiery dragons** were seen **flying** in the sky. A great **famine (hunger) soon followed** these signs ...

Fiery dragons and other monsters must have featured frequently in the storytelling of OE communities. One very famous man-eating monster is Grendel in the epic poem *Beowulf*. Like other Anglo-Saxon texts, it is difficult to read in its original form, but as with the *Anglo-Saxon Chronicle*, we can occasionally see and hear the seeds of our modern English vocabulary.

We have spent some time looking at the Anglo-Saxon era and OE, and of course that is not the whole story of English vocabulary, but we conclude this section with a quotation from the linguists David Denison and Richard Hogg, who state:

> If we trace history back, then, wherever English is spoken today, whether it be in Bluff, New Zealand, or Nome, Alaska, in every case its ultimate origins lie in Anglo-Saxon England.
>
> (Denison and Hogg 2006:3)

MORE INCOMERS

VIKINGS

The cruel omens and sheets of lightning recorded by the writer of the *Anglo-Saxon Chronicle* were a prelude to raids by Vikings on the north-eastern coasts of England, and the areas colonized by Vikings, the *Danelaw*, where the laws of the Danes held sway, were also important in terms of influences on the English language during the ninth and tenth centuries, mostly visible nowadays in northern English place-names of Scandinavian origin (e.g., *Whitby, Barnby, Mickleby* – in modern Swedish, *by* means 'village'). There are also a number of other words whose origin is Old Norse (ON) (the language of the Scandinavian Vikings) which are still heard in some English dialects and in standard English, such as *to flit* (meaning to move house – modern Danish *flytte*), *kid* (young animal or human), *lass* (girl), *to lake* (to play – modern Swedish *leka*), *law* (rules – modern Danish and Norwegian *lov*), *meek* (gentle/courteous), *saga* (a narrative), and *to thrive* (to grow/develop).

INFORMATION ADD-ON

Place names in England are a great source of information on the language as it was centuries ago, since the names of many towns and villages, although they have changed over the centuries, retain elements of OE and ON. The *Key to English Place-Names* at the University of Nottingham, UK, allows you to search for the name of a town or village and instantly gives brief information about the origin of the name.

This is the entry for the town of Scunthorpe in Northern England:

Scunthorpe

'Skuma's outlying farm/settlement'
  Elements and their meanings

- pers. n. (Old Norse) pers. n. Personal name
- Þorp (Old Norse) A secondary settlement, a dependent outlying farmstead or hamlet

The suffix -thorpe (Þorp) occurs in other place names in England, e.g., *Armthorpe, Bishopthorpe, Countesthorpe, Ingoldisthorpe, Mablethorpe*, and *Trusthorpe*.

The *Key to English Place-Names* can be accessed at http://kepn.nottingham.ac.uk/

The linguist David Crystal gives examples of ON and OE words which existed side-by-side where both forms have survived in present-day English, such as *dike* (ON) and *ditch* (OE), *sick* (ON) and *ill* (OE), and *skin* (ON) and *hide* (OE) (Crystal 2005: 74). Crystal also points out that ON vocabulary spread gradually southward in England over the course of two centuries during what is termed the Middle English period (Crystal 2005: 82). Middle English refers to English during the twelfth to the fifteenth century.

However, before they could sweep across the entire country, the Danes were pushed back by the Anglo-Saxon King Alfred the Great, who reigned during the latter art of the ninth century. Writing about King Alfred, the British historian Michael Wood makes the point that the English language might be quite different today if the Danes had conquered all of England (Wood 2005: chapter 5). But just before the twelfth century, British society was changed radically by the next wave of newcomers.

A BIG CHANGE: THE NORMANS ARRIVE

Although the vocabulary of English gradually evolved during the Anglo-Saxon period, it was when the French-speaking Normans arrived from Northern France in the eleventh century that things really changed. The famous battle of Hastings in 1066, a date imprinted on the minds of British people from their schooldays, in which the English king was killed, marked the beginning of the end of old Anglo-Saxon England. However, a single battle does not change a language overnight, and the transition from OE to what we call Middle English was gradual, as was the transition out of it, into Modern English. What is noteworthy is that medieval texts (broadly those of the twelfth to the fifteenth centuries) become much more recognizable to the modern eye and ear than OE ones.

Gerry Knowles, in his book about the evolution of English, tells us that English and French were in close contact with each other for more than 300 years in the medieval period which followed the Norman conquest, that the Norman conquerors became integrated with the native English, and that bilingualism was probably widespread (Knowles 1997: 46–47). English vocabulary became more diverse, with French words growing in frequency because of their use in the law and official business alongside Latin. Knowles also points out that French influenced the spelling of English so that words which might have been less obvious to our modern eye now became more transparent (p. 49).

French influence on English vocabulary has been long-lasting. The *Oxford English Dictionary* (OED) lists more than 500 words which entered English from Old French or Anglo-Norman during the half century from 1200 to 1250. Table 2.1 gives some familiar examples. By the late fourteenth century, the number of French imports peaked at over 2,800, declined a little as English began to be used more and more in official and learned contexts, but regularly maintained numbers over a 1,000 per annum over the next 500 years. French words were here to stay.

Table 2.1 Words of Anglo-Norman/Old French origin 1200–1250.

acquaintance	acquit	cellar	chamber
dangerous	false	familiar	general
heritage	image	large	lesson
matter	noble	park	reason
rob	sign	silence	term
treason	villainy	virtue	warrant

(Source *OED Online*, Oxford University Press, June 2021).[1]

PUTTING IT IN BLACK AND WHITE

So far, we have discussed manuscripts which show us different stages in the evolution of English vocabulary. The manuscripts were painstakingly written and copied by hand in beautiful script, often with colourful pictures and decorations ('illuminated' manuscripts). But what happens if, instead of only a single manuscript which has to be laboriously copied by hand, hundreds of copies could be turned out by a relatively simple machine – the printing press? The invention of printing was to have a profound influence on the evolution of English vocabulary.

At the beginning of this book, we mentioned the problems associated with defining an apparently straightforward word such as 'English'. English has never been a monolithic, single-voiced language. We know that it has always had dialects in which words have different forms or are differently pronounced and can be spelt differently from how they are used in neighbouring regions, whether in Old and Middle English or Modern English. Nonetheless, speakers of different English dialects can usually understand one another with minimal effort despite variations in grammar, vocabulary, and pronunciation. However, if you are a printer, you want to settle on just one consistent spelling, one set of grammatical conventions, and one variety of words in which to print your books, for obvious reasons of economy and common sense. You would not want to put in the same sentence three or four different dialect words for a loaf of bread every time you mentioned it. You had to choose. Printing played an important role in the emergence of a **standard English**, a variety that would appeal to the mercantile and gentrified classes of London and which would sow the seeds of the vocabulary we consider to be 'standard' nowadays, as used in education, the media, official communications, etc.

TELLING TALES

Printing was introduced to England by William Caxton. Caxton favoured the French-influenced English of London, which was growing in economic, social, and political importance. His most famous publication was Geoffrey Chaucer's *Canterbury Tales*, a series of oral narratives told by members of a motley group of pilgrims over a five-day journey from London to a Christian shrine in Canterbury, southern England. It is a wonderful source of English vocabulary, not only for its description of the season and the journey but also for the depiction of the men and women who take part in it. As one editor of the *Tales* says:

> It is the concise portrait of an entire nation, high and low, old and young, male and female, lay and clerical, learned and ignorant, rogue and righteous, land and sea, town and country...
>
> (Coghill 2003: xvii)

Figure 2.3, from William Caxton's 1485 edition of the *Tales*, showing the pilgrims all together at table, uniquely captures that social mix of characters who tell their stories.

Figure 2.3 The Canterbury pilgrims dine and tell their tales. Image © British Library Board G.11586, f.c4.

Caxton's first and second editions of the *Tales* published in 1476 and 1483 are held in the British Library. In his preface to the 1483 edition, Caxton heaps praise on Chaucer's contribution to the English language, which he made more beautiful, and which, before Chaucer, Caxton claimed, was rude and incongruous:

> ... we ought to give a singular laud unto that noble and great philosopher Geoffrey Chaucer, the which for his ornate writing in our tongue may well have the name of a laureate poet. For to-fore that he by labour embellished, ornated, and made fair our English, in this realm was had rude speech and incongruous ...
> (The British Library G.11586 Geoffrey Chaucer, *The Canterbury Tales*, 2nd edition [Westminster: William Caxton, 1483]).[2]

Generations of school students have studied the *Tales* and doubtless some have found them more difficult than others as regards their readability without a modern English translation, but whoever studies them must be struck by the number of familiar-looking words, albeit with unfamiliar spellings. The prologue to the *Tales* begins with a description of the English spring:

Whan that Aprille with his shoures sote	In April, when sweet showers fall,
The droghte of Marche hath perced to the rote,	And have pierced to the root he drought of March
And bathed every veyne in swich licour,	And bathed every vein in such liquor
Of which vertu engendred is the flour;	As engenders the flower
(The Project Gutenberg eBook of *The Complete Works of Geoffrey Chaucer*, Volume 4. *The Canterbury Tales*: ll. 1–4.)	

PIERS PLOWMAN

Chaucer was not the only writer whose work in English around the end of the fourteenth century has come down to us as a significant document for understanding the evolution of the language. Chaucer's contemporary, William Langland, wrote the allegorical long poem *The Vision of Piers Plowman*. It achieved popularity in its time, just as Chaucer's *Tales* did. It is another work wherein we can see many words familiar to us today, for example, in the opening lines of the *Prologue* to the poem. As does Chaucer, Langland begins with a seasonal setting:

In a somer seson, whan softe was the sonne	In a summer season when the sun was soft,
I shoop me into shroudes as as y shepherde were,	I dressed up as if I were a shepherd,
In habite as an heremite unholy of werkes,	In the unholy habit of a hermit,
Wente wide in this worle wondres to here.	Went out into the wide world to hear wonders
(The Project Gutenberg eBook of *The Vision and Creed of Piers Ploughman*, Volume I, by William Langland: ll. 1–8)	

Amongst other things, *Piers Plowman* contains a great amount of Latin alongside the English, in the form of verses, proverbs, and biblical quotations, showing how Latin continued to operate at the centre of the upper levels of society in Medieval England. One scholar commenting on the sociolinguistic background to the poem says:

> Latin was reserved for ideologically powerful institutions and discourses, such as the church, the universities, biblical exegesis, theology, philosophy, and commentaries of all kinds. The domains of English, on the other hand, had traditionally been ephemeral, such as popular lyrics, romances, and histories, as well as the overwhelming majority of day-to-day conversations.
>
> (Machan 1994: 361)

Not only does this remind us of the continued influence of Latin on English but we are also reminded that almost everything we say about the evolution of English vocabulary for most of the history of English from its Anglo-Saxon beginnings till the invention of sound recording in the twentieth century needs must be based on the written language. The vocabulary of everyday conversation – the activity that most people engage in most of the time – may be only palely reflected in the written works which historians of the language have at their disposal.

The manuscripts and early printing I have cited were mostly 'high art'– the poetry of *Piers Plowman* and *The Canterbury Tales* give us a particular type of vocabulary, but I tried to choose passages that depicted relatively ordinary scenes, and we also looked at *The Anglo-Saxon Chronicle* to sample different contexts for vocabulary. Naturally, sources for the earliest stages of English are limited, but we can nonetheless get a flavour for how the vocabulary of many centuries ago is related to the words and expressions we use today.

REFLECTION POINT

Look at this extract from the beginning of *The Miller's Tale* in Chaucer's *Canterbury Tales*. How many words look familiar in terms of modern-day English vocabulary? The story tells of a rich old man (*him* in the first line) who took in a lodger.

(Some clues: *povre* = poor; *or elles* = or else; *demen* = deem; *rekene* = recount/describe)

With him ther was dwellinge a povre scoler,
Had lerned art, but al his fantasye
Was turned for to lerne astrologye,
And coude a certeyn of conclusiouns
To demen by interrogaciouns,
If that men axed him in certein houres,
Whan that men sholde have droghte or elles shoures,
Or if men axed him what sholde bifalle
Of every thing, I may nat rekene hem alle.
                    (The Project Gutenberg eBook of The Complete Works of
                        Geoffrey Chaucer, Volume 4. The Canterbury Tales: ll.
                                                            3190–3198).[3]

INTO THE MODERN ERA

LANGUAGE ABOUT LANGUAGE

The start of the Early Modern era of English is usually dated to around 1480, which coincides with the advent of printing. The era lasted for almost 200 years before what scholars refer to as Modern

English, the English we can read easily today. During the Early Modern period, not only were important works written in English which have come down to us at the present day, but also scholars began more and more to record facts about the language. Grammars and dictionaries of English were born.

INFORMATION ADD-ON

In 1499, a grammar of Latin, written in English, was published. It is interesting to see how many words are familiar to us as students of English, even though the spelling has changed. Here we see a list of the eight parts of speech (or 'parts of reason') which grammarians were generally agreed upon. *Accedence* [*accidence* in modern spelling] refers to the study of grammatical inflections (see Chapter 1).

Accedence

How many partis of reason ben there (eyght) whiche bin **Nowne/** **Pronowne/Verbe/Adverbe/Partycyple/Coiunccion/preposicion/** **Interieccyo**
(noun, pronoun, verb, adverb, participle, conjunction, preposition, interjection)

Source: Oxford, Bodleian Library Arch. G e.4.[4]

One of the most important sources for the study of the vocabulary of any language are its grammars and dictionaries, and it was during the Early Modern era that the first monolingual English dictionary was published, in 1604. Its title was:

Table Alphabeticall, containing and teaching the true writing and understanding of hard usual English Words, borrowed from the Hebrew, Greeke, Latine, or French, &c.

This dictionary is a record of around 3,000 words in circulation at that time, along with simple definitions, so it is a window into the words its author observed to be in widespread use (*usual* words). The dictionary's author, Robert Cawdrey, was writing at a time when borrowed words from other languages were creating a layer of vocabulary that was opaque and difficult for the general population. We will return to Cawdrey's dictionary in Chapter 6. The linguistic historian Dieter Kastovsky says of the Early Modern period:

> The extensive borrowing from Latin and French brings about an increased dissociation of the vocabulary, i.e. fewer and fewer semantically related words are also formally morphologically related on the basis of transparent word-formation patterns. This increased and partly exaggerated borrowing also starts the controversy about 'hard words' or 'inkhorn terms', i.e. learned words that average people without a classical education would not understand.

> (Kastovsky 2006: 257)

AN EXPANDING VOCABULARY

Robert Cawdrey wanted his dictionary to bridge the vocabulary gap for a gentrified and commercial class faced with the expansion of science and academic study and a massive increase of borrowed words from French, Latin and Greek in the sixteenth century. Table 2.2 gives examples of Latin-based words entering English during the period 1500–1600 with meanings and senses we are familiar with today.

We can see from this selection that the Latin borrowings are principally abstract words or words connected with science and learning, as this was an age of great intellectual and cultural expansion, often called the English Renaissance, marked by major works of literature, music, and architecture.

Table 2.2 Words of Latin origin acquiring wider usage in the period 1600–1700.

abbreviate	academic	canal	cylinder
debilitate	definite	generate	globe
hereditary	illuminate	malevolent	map
notorious	ominous	parasite	reality
relaxation	sarcasm	verbatim	veteran

(Source: *OED Online*, Oxford University Press, August 2021).[5]

CIRCLING THE WORLD

The linguist Philip Gooden says, writing about English in the sixteenth to seventeenth century, during the reign of Queen Elizabeth I:

> In the Elizabethan period the English language flexes its muscles. It begins to experiment, to play around, to show off. It finds innovative ways of saying old things. It creates fresh expressions.
>
> (Gooden 2011: 85)

This was an era of expansion in trade and overseas adventure; the explorer Francis Drake sailed around the word, and imperial and colonizing ambitions came to the fore in England and elsewhere. The seeds were sown for English ultimately to become a world language. Flexing its muscles in the case of English vocabulary was seen in the introduction of new Latin-based words, some of which have survived, others not. The most famous figure of the period, William Shakespeare, certainly flexed the muscles of the vocabulary, and his plays and poems have given us many expressions still in use today. The expansion of printing meant that standardization in spelling increased, such that printed documents of the era now become much easier for our modern eyes to decipher; the vocabulary becomes familiar.

INFORMATION ADD-ON

The following expressions all appear in Shakespeare's works and are still widely in use today, though many English speakers may not think of them as centuries old or connected with Shakespeare's time.

melt/vanish into thin air   *kill with kindness*   *wild goose chase*

green-eyed monster   *break the ice*   *wear your heart upon your sleeve*

a heart of gold   *one fell swoop*   *too much of a good thing*

Although Shakespeare's plays depicted the lives of emperors, monarchs, and legendary characters and were therefore elevated and solemn in style, he also portrayed characters from the so-called lower classes. His occasional mockery of the way his characters used words was frequently humorous. The Shakespeare scholar Norman Blake, in his dictionary of informal language used by Shakespeare's characters when they are in 'relaxed, angry or teasing frame of mind', offers us 'colloquialisms reflecting non-standard or informal pronunciation, discourse and pragmatic markers, exclamations, oaths and words of abuse; clichés, traditional expressions and slang' (Blake 2004: 3). This is important for our understanding of English vocabulary because, until Shakespeare's time, we had little evidence of the vocabulary of ordinary, everyday language. In Blake's dictionary, we find a wealth of phrasal verbs (e.g., in the entry for *about: come about, hang about, hover about, peep about, set about*), which nicely counterbalances the idea that Shakespeare's vocabulary was all high-flown and classical.

It may not be that Shakespeare invented all the words and expressions first found in his works: some he did invent, others he took from the vocabulary which was in use at the time. The OED contains more than 1,000 words which were first evidenced in Shakespeare's works. Shakespeare was certainly an innovator who left his mark on the English language. His life and times represent a key period in the expansion of the English vocabulary. Modern English, as know it today, had begun.

The Renaissance was an era of great progress in the arts and sciences. Scientific and cultural upheavals bring with them the need for new words, new terms to express new meanings. There was considerable debate as to whether the necessary vocabulary should be borrowed from Latin and Greek or developed from the vernacular English. Latin won out. More than 10,000 new words and terms of Latin origin are recorded in the OED for the period 1550–1650. Some of these did not survive to our present time, others did, including *abducted, ab initio, canine, edible, germinate, gesticulate, marital, nascent, nauseate, pantomime, sanctimonious,* and *validate.*

The seventeenth-century poet John Milton, author of the epic poem *Paradise Lost*, is said to have contributed more than 600 words to the English vocabulary; his Cambridge alma mater, Christ's College, lists on its website many of the words and expressions Milton is considered to have added to our vocabulary[6]. The most famous English translation of the Bible, the King James version of 1611, is also commonly held to have been responsible for a number of expressions which are still in widespread use today, even though we may not be aware of it. David Crystal, discussing the idiom *a fly in the ointment*, says:

> Not many know, and only etymologists care, that *a fly in the ointment* comes from Ecclesiastes*. Foreign learners of English would simply pick it up as an idiom, along with *kick the bucket* and all the other expressions that have nothing to do with the Bible at all. Their religious beliefs are neither here nor there. Indeed, they may have no religious belief of any kind. Yet the biblical expression will be part of their English language ability.
>
> (Crystal 2010: 5) [*one of the books of the Old Testament]

Crystal's most generous assessment, depending on how you count them, is that there are some 257 idiomatic expressions still in use, either directly or creatively exploited and manipulated in some way in present-day English either from the King James Bible or other similar biblical translations. The OED uses more than 4,000 quotations from the King James Bible and many of these are the first in a word's entry in the dictionary or the first example of a particular meaning. For instance, the meaning of *ambassador* in the present-day expression *goodwill ambassador* comes from the King James Bible, as do *(hiding/covering) a multitude of sins*, *to cut (something/somebody) short*, and *to see/think fit (to do something)*.

As with Shakespeare's works, the King James Bible influenced English vocabulary, thanks to printing and a growing literate population. In the case of the Bible, its official status as the version to be read in churches guaranteed it widespread circulation, but it also circulated around the world on the back of trade, colonization, and the spread of English missionary work and education. As the globe shrank, the reach of English expanded.

A SETTLED LANGUAGE

SPELLING IT OUT

It may seem odd to jump from the time of Shakespeare to the present, but it is often rightly said that English has not changed greatly over the last 400 years. We can follow Shakespeare's plays in the original with not too much effort in terms of recognising words, even though we may find his plots and ideas complex and challenging. Books, newspapers, and magazines of the eighteenth, nineteenth, and twentieth centuries present even less of a challenge in terms of their vocabulary. That is not to say that the vocabulary has not evolved but, compared to the upheavals in the language brought about by invaders and conquerors over the centuries since the arrival of the Romans, the basic fabric of our present-day vocabulary has been with us for a very long time.

What changes have there been to our vocabulary? For one thing, spelling became standardized over the centuries since Shakespeare's time, mostly thanks to the invention of printing and the subsequent growth of printed media (books, newspapers, public and official documents). Barber, Beal, and Shaw (2012: 213) point out that there were at least five different ways of spelling the name Shakespeare in circulation during Shakespeare's time! They also give examples of the way English spelling became 'stuck' thanks to standardization. The spelling of many words remained unchanged, while the pronunciation shifted; for example, the silent *-gh-* in *knight* represents an earlier pronunciation, as does the *w-* in *wrong* and the *k-* in *knee* (compare the modern Swedish word for 'knee', *knä*, where the *k* is pronounced).

NEW WORLDS, NEW CULTURES

As we saw in Chapter 1 in connection with loanwords, the growth of overseas trade and imperial adventurism brought the English language into contact with new and different cultures, and that process of broadening cultural horizons has since been added to by travel and tourism. The last several centuries have brought words connected with the natural world, food and drink, music and dance, sports and fashion, and other domains of social and cultural experience into English. Words and expressions like *tango, boules, chauffeur, gamelan, cava, parmesan, gnu, chorizo, taramosalata, muntjac, haute couture, off-piste, know-tow,* and *en route,* along with many more from a wide range of languages, have made it into English dictionaries over the relatively recent past.

NEW TECHNOLOGIES, NEW ENGLISHES

The centuries since Shakespeare's time have seen an explosion of new technologies, from book printing to newspapers and magazines and websites, from the telephone to gramophone records to digital audio recording and smartphones, from photography and cinema to TV and internet streaming, from the postal and telegraph service to email and social media. At the same time, means of transport from sophisticated sailing vessels and steamships to railways, motor vehicles, and aeroplanes have shrunk the world and provided mobility and contact between peoples on a scale never seen before. All of these have changed and influenced our vocabulary.

> **REFLECTION POINT**
>
> Consider some of the vocabulary which we use in our everyday lives now which would not have existed 100 years ago – words and expressions connected with communication, or travel, or music, or work, for example.

Electronic communications of various kinds have given a recent boost to the vocabulary, with all the words and expressions connected with computing and social media becoming part of our daily lives, for example, *mouse, download, upload, tweet, spreadsheet, streaming, keyboard, online, internet, screen-grab, posting, memory stick, app, username, ping, meme, doom-scrolling, algorithm, email, e-book,* and blends such as *blog* (web + log) and *webinar* (web + seminar), all formed from words and morphemes already existing but combined in new ways to encode our new technological experiences.

Most significantly, the shrinking globe and an educated, mobile population has wrested English from the control of its original colonial and trading owners and made the language the property of the world, a **lingua franca** (a language used between parties none of whom may be native speakers of that language). English words and expressions have found their way into other languages to an extent never seen before. Swedish and Danish detective and political thriller TV series achieved great popularity in the UK in the first decades of this century; to an increasing extent, they contain frequent use of English words and expressions, most notably taboo words, dropped into the script; French too has adopted a number of English words and expressions.

Meanwhile, the old 'motherland' English inculcated through schooling in colonial settings has evolved into robust and independent local varieties with their own vocabulary suited to the needs of their societies and their contact with neighbouring cultures. These **world Englishes** stand on their own feet and often give new words back to the old colonial and economically dominant powers; the traffic has certainly not been one-way. The *OED* has many hundreds of words and phrases from countries where English was a colonizing language where a local English vocabulary has grown independently. We return to this theme in Chapter 6.

INFORMATION ADD-ON

Here are some words and phrases from English-speaking countries and regions where English was a colonial import and/or where world Englishes have emerged. All of these are in the *OED*.

Add oil! (term of encouragement) Hong Kong
agric (improved/genetically modified crop) Nigeria
hawker centre (street food stalls) Singapore, Malaysia
big-eye (greedy) Caribbean
yachtie (yachtsman/woman) Australia, New Zealand
upgradation (raised level/status) India

In October 2021, the American *Merriam-Webster Dictionary* added 455 new words in just that one month alone.[7] These are listed under different headings, including online culture and communication, coronavirus-related words, technology and science, politics, food, medicine, and pop culture. Some of them are foreign loanwords; others follow the usual pattern of rearrangements and new meanings for existing words and morphemes. We may confidently predict that October 2021 was not a one-off and that English vocabulary will continue to reflect new realities. Meanwhile, old words will die out, meanings will change and become obsolete, though old words may cling on in regional dialects, caught up in a natural process of evolution and the survival of the fittest. We cannot fully understand English vocabulary if we only take a snapshot at any one moment in its long history – being prepared to delve into the past, to grapple with texts and words which look unfamiliar to our modern eye and to trace their journey over the centuries, helps us unlock the treasure house of the English lexicon.

In the next chapter, we ask some basic questions about meaning and how all the many thousands of words in English are related (or unrelated) to one another. Later, in Chapter 6, we consider how the vast network of English vocabulary is put into service to create what we mean by the words we use in our social lives.

FURTHER READING

Baker, P. S. 2012. *Introduction to Old English*. Third edition. Chichester: Wiley-Blackwell.
This is a good, clear introduction to Old English which takes the reader through its history, grammar, vocabulary, spelling, and pronunciation and literary style. It does not assume any prior knowledge of Old English and also offers an introduction to basic grammatical terms. It includes an anthology section of Old English texts.

Crystal, D. 2005. *The Stories of English*. London: Penguin Books.
Any book about the English language by David Crystal is worth reading. He is one of the foremost linguists of his generation and he writes in a clear, accessible style. In this book, he takes the reader from the origins of English through to the world dominance of the language in our time.

Knowles, G. 1997. *A Cultural History of the English Language*. London: Arnold.
Gerry Knowles' book takes us through the long history of the English Language from its Anglo-Saxon origins to the present day, covering social and cultural change as well as linguistic evolution. It is clearly written and full of illustrative examples of vocabulary, grammar, spelling, and pronunciation.

NOTES

1 www.oed.com/search?dateFilter=1200-1249&langClass=-French&page=1&scope=ENTRY&timeline=true&type=dictionarysearch.

2   www.bl.uk/collection-items/william-caxton-and-canterbury-tales.

3   www.gutenberg.org/files/22120/22120-h/22120-h.htm#miller.

4   https://digital.bodleian.ox.ac.uk/objects/7ae0f420-beff-45e0-9cfc-7ccbb20671d1/.

5   www.oed.com/search?browseType=sortAlpha&browseValue=v&case-insensitive=true&dateFilter=1500-1600&langClass=Latin&nearDistance=1&obsolete=false&ordered=false&page=8&pageSize=20&scope=SENSE&sort=entry&type=dictionarysearch.

6   https://www.christs.cam.ac.uk/why-milton-matters#english.

7   https://www.merriam-webster.com/words-at-play/new-words-in-the-dictionary.

WHAT DOES IT ALL MEAN?

FROM FORM TO MEANING

If we speak a language as our native tongue, we know what the words we use and hear in everyday life mean. Now and again, we will come across words we've never heard before or are not sure of, but we can easily solve the problem by looking things up in a dictionary. The dictionary will tell us what the word means by giving a definition and often some examples of its use. Alongside all the tens of thousands of words in circulation in everyday life, there are thousands of other highly specific scientific and technical terms whose meanings we may need never bother to learn unless our careers demand it. But what does it involve to say that word x *means* such-and-such? In Chapters 1 and 2, we were mostly concerned with the forms of the vocabulary, its words and how they are composed, how they combine to form compounds and multi-word expressions and so on, and how and why they have changed over the centuries. All these many forms constitute what we generally call the **lexicon** of English. However, when we turn to what and how all those forms carry meaning, we enter the world of **semantics**, the study of meaning.

WORDING THE WORLD

The basic function of words is to encode our experiences of the world. We can experience the world in a multitude of different ways, both concrete and abstract – we can accidentally cut our finger with a kitchen knife or get wet in the rain, but we can also share ideas and concepts with others and make judgements and have opinions. We have conceptual and scientific knowledge of the world around us, often called **encyclopaedic knowledge**. We know that the word *roots* refers to the underground growth of plants and trees. We know that *green* refers to a particular colour of light on the spectrum and we use it to refer to the light reflected from growing plants or any other object that reflects that colour. These are the **core**, basic meanings of the words *roots* and *green*; it is what the words **denote**. **Denotation** is a basic feature of meaning. It is how we word our worlds. The forms (the words themselves) are like bridges; they link the world to concepts in our minds. Denotation is what writers of dictionaries (**lexicographers**) set out to record.

The linguist David Singleton warns us, however, to be wary of associating a simple triangle between a phenomenon in the real word, a word or expression, and a mental concept. He says:

> One difficulty with this kind of representation is that, in implying that each particular form is uniquely associated with a single particular concept, it fails to provide any account of cases where more than one expression is associated with a single meaning or of cases where a single expression is associated with more than one meaning ...
>
> Singleton (2016: 65)

In other words, there is often more than one word or expression available to refer to the same thing. *Problem*, *difficulty*, and *issue* can all refer to the same situation of something being not easy to understand or resolve. And vice-versa, one word or expression can denote more than one thing: a *bank* may be the edge of a river or a financial institution.

Some words do have a direct relationship to something in the real world. The word *brachiosaurus* refers to a specific type of herbivorous dinosaur that once existed; it is hard to imagine the word having any other meaning or any other context of use. But apart from highly specific technical and scientific words, most everyday words in English have more than one meaning over and above what a dictionary-writer might consider to be their core meanings (their denotation). For example, the verb *get* in *get a newspaper, get*

REFLECTION POINT

What do you call this article of clothing? Consider other clothes you wear. Do they have more than one name?

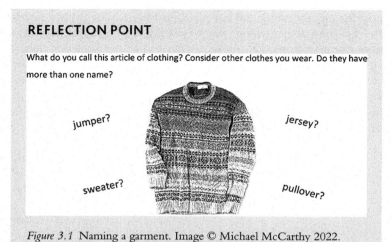

jumper?

jersey?

sweater?

pullover?

Figure 3.1 Naming a garment. Image © Michael McCarthy 2022.

an email, get angry, and *get the door* all seem to refer to quite different actions and processes.

If *brachiosaurus* just refers to one very specific type of animal and nothing else, we can say that the word is **monosemous** – it just has one meaning. The verb *get,* on the other hand, seems to have many meanings (receive, buy, become, respond to, etc.); it is **polysemous**. **Polysemy** is the norm, especially in the case of everyday words, and monosemous words are rare outside of highly specific scientific and technical nomenclature.

The various names for the woollen garment in the picture are not an isolated or special case. As mentioned above, on many occasions we will have the choice of saying *problem, difficulty,* or *issue* to refer to exactly the same negative feature of a situation. Equally, we have to account for being able to say *it's not easy/not straightforward* instead of *it's difficult/problematic,* with more or less the same meaning. What is more, we shall have to take into account the fact that two of the words we discussed above, *roots* and *green,* not only denote parts of plants and a colour on the spectrum. People can have roots (where they came from, where their family and heritage are located, etc.) and a person may be *green with envy,* or *green* in the sense of 'inexperienced'; one's politics may be *green* in the sense of prioritizing environmental concerns, or one may have *green fingers* and be good at gardening. So, words not only denote, they also have **connotations**, i.e., meanings derived from their core, denotative meanings, meanings which encode social or cultural values or emotive attitudes which we interpret in context and because of our knowledge of collocations and fixed expressions. Connotation is just as important as denotation. One of the foremost linguists to study the lexicon, Adrienne Lehrer, put it this way:

> Emotive meaning, association, and connotation have been reluctantly acknowledged by philosophers of language as existing, but then ignored or relegated to pragmatics or literary studies. Nonetheless, these factors play an important role in language sense and language use.
>
> (Lehrer 2012: 104)

John Lyons, in his huge two-volume work on semantics, also discusses the question of denotation and connotation (Lyons 1977: 174–176).

MAKING SENSE OF THE LEXICON

Because it is quite difficult or impossible to match most English words with a one-to-one relationship to real-world phenomena, we can instead consider how words relate to *one another*. Linguists do this by attempting to organize words into **lexical fields**, that is to say groupings of words which have properties in common. Sometimes what they have in common is that they are very close in meaning, sometimes that they are opposite in meaning, or sometimes that they belong to the same 'family tree', with words above them that act like parents and grandparents. How words relate to one another, rather than how they relate to the real world, is called **sense relations**.

The lexical fields themselves must, of course, be related not just through structural relations but through meanings in the world; otherwise, just saying that two words are similar or opposite in meaning would be a rather pointless exercise, so we say that lexical fields encode the meanings contained in **semantic fields**. The linguists Adrienne Lehrer and Eva Kittay explain the theory behind the idea of semantic fields:

> Semantic field theory makes a meaning claim that the meanings of words must be understood, in part, in relation to other words that articulate a given content domain and that stand in the relation of affinity and contrast to the word(s) in question.
>
> (Kittay and Lehrer 1992/2009: 3–4)

An example of a semantic field would be TEMPERATURE. In the natural world, temperature is a continuum; it is we humans who divide it up into degrees (whether Fahrenheit, Celsius, or other systems of measurement) and it is we humans who decide whether something is 'cold' or 'hot' or somewhere in between. We divide the semantic space into compartments which are the sections of the lexical field and agree on words for those sections. English words to fill the different sections of the TEMPERATURE field include *freezing, cold, tepid, lukewarm, warm, hot, boiling, sizzling, torrid,* and so on. All the words for describing degrees of heat and cold taken together constitute a **lexical set**.

Just because English partitions a semantic field in a particular way does not mean English has a grasp on 'logic' or 'objectivity'. Different cultures may respond to their environments by dividing up the temperature continuum in a different way, resulting in a different lexical set. Differences in semantic fields and the lexical sets associated with them often become apparent when we compare languages. So, French and Spanish, for instance, distinguish between 'knowing' a person, as in *connaître* (Fr.)/*conocer* (Sp.), and knowing a fact or idea, as in *savoir* (Fr.)/*saber* (Sp.). Similarly, the single notion of 'thinking' in English is divided into three types of mental activity in Swedish, with three different verbs, covered by just one in English. The Swedish verbs distinguish between *think* meaning hold an opinion or judgement, *think* meaning expressing a degree of certainty or doubt, and *think* meaning to mentally ponder or use one's mind:

English	Swedish translation
I **think** she's coming today.	Jag **tror** att hon kommer idag.
I **think** it's a good idea.	Jag **tycker** det är en bra idé.
I **think** a lot about my future.	Jag **tänker** mycket på min framtid.

Semantic fields are not static or fixed forever; they change and evolve as our social experiences change. An example of a recent shift in a semantic field is words related to human sex and gender. As society has become more open and inclusive concerning such matters, the simple binary distinction between *male/female, man/woman, he/she*, etc. has shifted to admit words that describe people's non-binary choices, so, for example, new pronouns such as *ze* and *hir* have appeared in English to attempt to fill the new semantic space that has opened up between *he* and *she* (for further discussion and examples, see my book on grammar in this series: McCarthy 2021b: 178–180). And words can hop from one space to another to do service in expressing new realities: *mouse* has long occupied one space in the field of RODENTS alongside *rats, squirrels, hamsters*, etc. *Mouse* was then borrowed to occupy a space in the field of COMPUTERS AND COMPUTING to describe the tool with which we navigate around a computer screen; *mouse* now sits alongside *keyboard, screen, memory stick, trackpad, router*, etc. *Mouse* now occupies a space in at least two semantic fields.

SAME OR DIFFERENT?

One of the basic ways in which the meanings of words relate to one another is the degree of similarity or difference among them. If I say 'It's time to start, so let's begin' you understand that *start* and *begin* mean more or less the same. If I say 'from start to finish' then you understand *start* and *finish* as being quite opposite in meaning to each other. When two or more words mean the same, we call it **synonymy** and we say that the words are **synonyms**. When they are opposite in meaning, we can call it **antonymy** and say that the words are **antonyms**. Synonymy and antonymy are two fundamental ways in which the lexicon is organized.

SYNONYMY

How do we know if two words are synonyms? We can answer the question by seeing if they are substitutable in context. If two words can be substituted for each other in the same context, we can say that they are synonymous. In our earlier examples with the verb *get*, we can see how *get* can be synonymous in context with *buy* (get a newspaper), *become* (get angry), *receive* (get an email), and so on. Context is the key to understanding synonymy. Meaning in context is often referred to as **pragmatic meaning**. Pragmatic meaning answers the question *What does the speaker/writer mean* by using this word in this context?

But what about words out of context? Are there pairs of words which are always synonymous, regardless of context? The answer is probably not. The historical linguist David Burnley, writing about Middle English, says:

> Although synonymy is the most familiar of the relations existing between the meanings of words, it must be recognised that it is, to be more precise, a relationship of sense; complete denotational sameness is rare, and rarer still is equivalence in terms of both semantic and pragmatic meaning.
>
> (Burnley 1992: 472)

Although some pairs of words can be substituted for each other in almost all contexts, it is usually the case that there will be one or more contexts where they cannot be exchanged. **Absolute** (sometimes called **complete**) **synonymy** probably does not exist. Even in examples such as *sofa* and *settee*, or the verbs *start* and *begin*, we find differences of **register** (e.g., degrees of formality, different usage among different social groups, speaking versus writing, etc.). In the British National Corpus (BNC) of 1994, *start* and *begin* as verbs are close in frequency in the written texts of the corpus, but in the 1994 spoken texts, *start* is seven times more frequent than *begin*. Register is not just a bolt-on-extra to the meaning of a word; a word's register is as much a part of its identity as its denotative meaning. *Kid*, *child*, and *offspring* can all refer to a young human, but their different degrees of formality is what makes them non-synonymous or at best only **near-synonyms**. Changes over time can also result in one of a pair of words which might fulfil the same meaning dropping out of usage: *looking-glass* and *mirror*, *wireless* and *radio*, *gramophone* and *record player*, *lodestone* and *magnet*, all at different points in their history could well have been considered alternatives, but today the first word in each pair sounds quaint and outdated. Some American English and British English words can refer to the same thing (e.g., the parts of a car – *trunk* versus *boot*, *hood* versus *bonnet*), so regional variation also plays a part in separating apparent synonyms. The semanticist Stephen Ullmann points out that even in cases where two technical terms are available to refer to the same invention, they tend eventually to be 'sorted out', i.e., one of the terms will drop out. He also states that absolute synonymy 'runs counter to our whole way of looking at language' (Ullmann 1962: 142).

To understand synonymy fully, we need to be aware of the history of English vocabulary and how it has evolved – that is one of the reasons why we needed the historical narrative in Chapter 2. At different points over the centuries, French, Latin, and Greek have contributed learned and technical words which have found their place alongside words of Anglo-Saxon origin, producing a 'parallel' vocabulary, where the imported words tend to be longer, more confined to scholastic and scientific usage, and more formal. Ullmann (1962: 146) gives pairs of words where the first is from Old English and the second is a scholastic import, for example, *bodily/ corporeal, brotherly/fraternal, answer/reply, fiddle/violin,* and *help/aid.*

INFORMATION ADD-ON

Some pairs of words available as synonyms are contrasted through their origin in Old English or Anglo-Norman French. For example, *begin* from Old English and *commence* from French are often interchangeable, albeit *commence* is the more formal of the two.

Further examples (OE= Old English; FR = French)

ghost (OE)/*phantom* (Fr)   *smell* (OE)/*odour* (Fr)   *fair* (OE)/*blonde* (Fr)
freedom (OE)/*liberty* (Fr)   *wild* (OE)/*savage* (Fr)   *wed* (OE)/*marry* (Fr)

One interesting question is why a language should have synonyms at all, even if they are only near-synonyms rather than absolute? Language is, generally speaking, economical, saying what it needs to say and no more, so why do we need more than one way of expressing exactly the same idea? We return to that question in Chapter 6, when we consider how people use and exploit vocabulary in everyday conversation.

LOOKS THE SAME, SOUNDS THE SAME, BUT ...

Some words in English look the same, that is they are spelt the same but have quite different meanings: *bass* (/bæs/ rhyming with *class*) is a type of fish; *bass* (/beɪs/ rhyming with *face*) is the lowest range of musical notes or a person who sings in that low range. The two words are **homographs**; they are written the same but pronounced differently and mean something different. Other examples are *row* (/rəʊ/ rhyming with *go*) meaning a line of something or to propel a boat using oars, and *row* (/raʊ/ rhyming with *now*) meaning a bad-tempered argument, and *minute* (/ˈmɪnɪt/ rhyming with *limit*) meaning 60 seconds and *minute* (/maɪˈnjuːt/ rhyming with *acute*) meaning very small.

Some words sound the same but are spelt differently and/or have different meanings. To *break* a glass is different from to *brake* suddenly in a car, to *sow* crops is different from to *sew* a button on a coat, the *bow* of a ship is different from the *bough* of a tree. In each pair, the words in italics are pronounced identically. These are **homophones**. There are usually historical reasons to do with how and when the words entered the language and the peculiarities of the history of English spelling (see Chapter 2) behind the apparent overlaps in homographs and homophones. The type of similarity seen in homographs and homophones is called **homonymy** (Figure 3.2).

Figure 3.2 Homographs: singing bass. © Jake Tebbit 2022.

SOMETHING DIFFERENT

Synonyms are words which are interchangeable, so you can be described as *happy* and *content* at the same time, or *anxious* and *worried* at the same time. But you can't be *alive* and *dead* at the same time, or *single* and *married* at the same time, you cannot *push* and *pull* something simultaneously, and something cannot be *a liquid* and *a solid* at the same time. Some pairs of words seem to be opposites of each other; they are **antonyms**. It may seem odd to say that oppositeness is based on similarity but it is clear that *single* and *married* share the property of 'civil status', *hot* and *cold* share the property of 'temperature', while pairs such as *egg* and *table-lamp*, *shower* and *dandelion* seem to have little or nothing in common and we could hardly conceive of them ever functioning as antonyms.

Not all opposites present an either/or option. We saw in the earlier discussion of the TEMPERATURE lexical field in English that the words *hot* and *cold* sit alongside a number of other words that refer to varying degrees of 'hotness' or 'coldness', such as *ice-cold, freezing, tepid, lukewarm, warm, boiling, torrid*, etc. *Hot* and *cold* are **gradable antonyms**: more or less of their qualities can be expressed, unlike **non-gradable antonyms** such as *dead* and *alive*, for which the Lyons prefers the term **complementaries** (Lyons 1977: 279). Someone can be *happier* or *sadder*, or *happiest* or *saddest*, but they cannot be *deader* or *most married*. If we say we are feeling *half dead* or *totally alive*, we are probably joking, emphasising a situation or expressing ourselves figuratively, not literally. Other lexical sets with graded differences in meaning include *to walk* and its opposite, on a scale of rapid motion involving the legs, *to run*, where a range of intermediate words are available such as *plod, stroll, amble, trot, canter*, and *gallop*, or on a scale of size from *small* to *big* we have *minuscule, tiny, minute, little, medium-sized, average-sized, large, big, huge, massive, gigantic, enormous*, etc.

Hot and *cold* seem to be the most basic core, benchmark or prototypical words on a scale of temperature differences. The core terms on various types of scales are considered as **canonical** antonyms by Jones et al. (2012). These are pairs of words which are psychologically embedded as opposites in people's minds, such as *old* and *young*, *hot* and *cold*, and *good* and *bad*. Around the canonical words, other words may express 'more' or 'less' or be somewhere in between. Thus, our TEMPERATURE words listed earlier could be expressed as a scale with *hot* and *cold* in canonical position.

ice-cold freezing **COLD** tepid lukewarm warm **HOT** boiling torrid

Our knowledge of such core antonyms is based on a mix of experience of the world, repeated exposure to the language, and/or sometimes the forms of the words themselves (e.g., *legal* versus *illegal*, *possible* versus *impossible*).

Another type of oppositeness can be observed in certain pairs of words. If you *sell* me something, I *buy* it. If you *lend* me something, I *borrow* it. If the bridge goes *over* the road, then the road goes *under* the bridge. If you are my *doctor/teacher*, I am your *patient/pupil*. These are **reciprocal** or **converse** antonyms; they work in both directions (Figure 3.3).

Most people are familiar with dictionaries; fewer people may have ever used a **thesaurus**, which is a kind of dictionary which gives lists of synonyms and antonyms instead of definitions. As I type this sentence, if I select with my mouse the word *select*, my

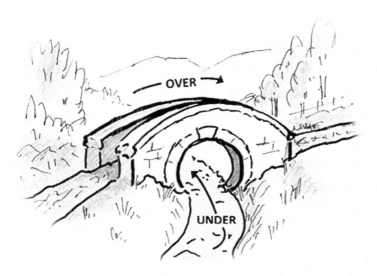

Figure 3.3 Reciprocal antonyms. Image © Michael McCarthy 2022.

word processing programme allows me to click on a 'thesaurus' option and then a list of synonyms pops up, offering me *pick, take, single out, opt*, and various other verbs which could possibly fit into my sentence instead of *select*. If I click on the word *include*, not only do I get synonyms such as *contain, embrace*, and *comprise*, the thesaurus also offers me *exclude, omit*, and *reject* as antonyms. A thesaurus is a powerful way of organizing how close or distant in meaning the words of a language are.

> **REFLECTION POINT**
>
> If you have a word processor which gives you a 'thesaurus' option, try selecting random words in any text you have written on your computer and see if the thesaurus provides synonyms and antonyms. Consider how suitable the offerings would be as replacements for words in your text.

CLASSIFYING THE WORLD

THE UPSIDE-DOWN TREE

There is another basic way in which words relate to one another, this time more like a family tree, or like the image of an upside-down tree in Figure 3.4, where big boughs divide off from the trunk and smaller branches grow from the boughs. The trunk of the tree represents the names of major classes of people, animals, and things in the world, for example, MAMMALS, or FISH, or FRUIT, or VEHICLES, or METALS, or VEGETABLES. These words can act as **superordinate** words in their class (sometimes called **hypernyms**). Above them there may be further, more general superordinate terms such as PLANT and ANIMAL. Below them, on the branches, are the words that name the different members of that class, for example, the superordinate FISH would include under its heading for most speakers of British English *cod, hake, mackerel, bream, salmon, bass, sardine, haddock*, etc. These are **co-hyponyms**, that is they exist on the same level of the family tree, like siblings. The relationship between co–hyponyms and superordinate words is one of **hyponymy**. Hyponymy is a way of

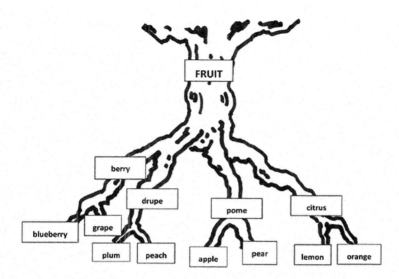

Figure 3.4 Hyponymy: the upside-down tree. Image © Michael McCarthy 2022.

classifying our world and our experiences into smaller and larger groups. Figure 3.4 shows one way of organizing different types of popular fruits.

SCIENTIFICALLY SPEAKING

Taxonomies or tree-diagrams of the type in Figure 3.4 are often drawn up by scientists to create strict classification systems. I am not a horticulturalist, but I like most kinds of fruit and I am familiar with all the names of the fruits along the bottom line of the diagram. Moving up the diagram, the terms *berry* and *citrus* are part of my vocabulary, but I have never before used the word *drupe* or *pome* and I will probably never need to use them outside of this book. Scientific taxonomies are a rather special example of hyponymy, but they do show us how hyponymy works: something can be a *berry*, but it can't be a *blueberry* and a *grape* at the same time, and it can't be a *drupe* and a *berry* at the same time. We can go up or down the tree, with different results. If a *blueberry* is a *berry*, and a berry is a fruit, then that **entails** (necessarily means) that a blueberry is also a fruit, but not vice-versa. Because something is a fruit, it does not entail that it is a *blueberry*.

We could turn the upside-down tree the right way up, with the roots of the tree in the ground and consider how the various fruits at the top of the tree may have adapted to their environment over millennia and evolved to become different from one another, all coming from some primordial organism FRUIT. The same logical conditions apply. Just because something is a fruit does not entail that it is a drupe, and if it is a drupe, it does not entail that it is a plum, and so on. As the linguist M. Lynne Murphy says of hyponymy, the relationship is 'hierarchical and asymmetrical' (Murphy 2003: 10).

Murphy makes a distinction between **taxonomic** hyponymy and **functional** hyponymy, in this way:

> Taxonomic relations are the IS-A-KIND-OF relation, whereas functional relations are the IS-USED-AS-A-KIND-OF relation. For example, *cow* is in a taxonomic relation to *animal* (a cow *is* an animal), but in a functional relation to *livestock* (a cow *functions as* livestock). The functional relation is more tenuous because it is not a logically necessary relation: not every cow is livestock; not every dog is a pet; ...
>
> (Murphy 2003: 220)

The hyponymy relation is most readily applicable to nouns and becomes more problematic if we try to apply it to, for example, adjectives: *crazy, silly, stupid,* and *daft* may be said to be 'ways of behaving' or 'features of a situation', in both cases under noun-phrase headings with no obvious adjective superordinate.

FUZZY BORDERS AND STEREOTYPES

We are not, most of us, botanists, zoologists, chemists, or biologists, so we work with much simpler systems of hyponymy in our everyday lives, which may be called **folk taxonomies**. Indeed, the tree in Figure 3.4 is only a partial view of the world of fruits and there are other ways of classifying them. For example, for most people, a *tomato* is a vegetable, though strictly speaking it is a fruit. And, as Lyons (1977: 293) points out, we are more likely to explain the term *bovine mammal* by giving *cow* as an example, rather than, vice-versa, explaining a *cow* to someone as a *bovine mammal*. I know what a *plum* and a *peach* are; I can conceive of them as examples of *drupes* to help me understand the unfamiliar superordinate, instead of vice-versa. Clearly, some words are more core than others in a taxonomy such as the upside-down tree of Figure 3.4. Core terms are the ones that spring to mind when we think of taxonomies; they 'stick out' from the rest; they are **salient**.

Hyponymy is often somewhat fuzzy and blurred round the edges, and people do not always agree on what should be included or not under a superordinate term. Consider the word *shop*. In late 2021, the UK government issued special regulations for England to counteract the increase in coronavirus cases. It was widely reported in the media that the new regulations included the obligation to wear a face covering 'in shops and on public transport'. Most people would agree on what public transport typically means (buses, trains, ferries) but what about taxis hailed in the street? And what does *shops* include? Large supermarkets, DIY stores, hairdressers, dry-cleaners, nail or tattoo parlours? Much debate and discussion could be had on these questions, and no two people may agree on exactly what a *shop* is.

REFLECTION POINT

How many of this list of words would you include as co-hyponyms of the term VEHICLE?

> *bus, van, lorry, bicycle, train, canoe, wheelbarrow, golf buggy, aeroplane, spaceship, car, raft, monocycle, ferryboat, sleigh, motorbike, electric bicycle, electric scooter, tractor, ride-on lawnmower*

For more examples of this type and for an extended discussion, see Rosch and Mervis (1975).

Despite the fuzziness of many everyday examples of hyponymy, most people agree on the core members of the list of possible co-hyponyms. So, in the world of *vehicles*, cars, buses, vans, and lorries are considered as **stereotypes** for the idea of VEHICLE, while golf-buggies and tractors might be more marginal in people's minds, and some items may be dismissed as falling outside of the concept of VEHICLE altogether (electric scooter? canoe?

monocycle?). Other examples of stereotypes might include one's typical image of a BIRD; for most people in the UK, it is more likely to be a robin, a sparrow or a blackbird than an emu, a pelican or a vulture, and a rose is more likely to act as a stereotype of FLOWER than a bird of paradise flower. The linguist Eleanor Rosch and her associates did a number of psychological experiments in the 1970s that showed that people could very quickly and confidently classify a sparrow as a bird but were more hesitant about including penguins in the category of BIRD (Rosch 1973, Rosch et al. 1976). Sparrows are **prototypical** birds for many people; they are the prototype bird, the one that best represents the BIRD category. This way of categorizing the world is seen as universal, albeit individual languages and cultures in different environments may generate different sets and prototypes:

> It is the principle of category formation that is claimed to be universal. On the most general level, categories form so as to be maximally differentiable from each other. This is accomplished by categories which have maximum cue validity - i.e., categories that have the most attributes common to members of the category and the least attributes shared with members of other categories.
>
> (Rosch et al. 1976: 435)

AN ARM AND A LEG: PARTS AND WHOLES

Hyponymy is a relationship of inclusion: *vehicle* includes *cars* in the list of co-hyponyms, and *car* includes *vehicle* as an element of its meaning. Another sort of inclusion is when we relate the parts of something to one another. *Engine, wheel, gearbox, clutch, radiator,* and *fuel tank* are not types of cars but are parts of a car. Taken all together, with all the other necessary parts (*coachwork, seats, exhaust system, windscreen,* etc.), they make up a car. This part–whole relationship is called **meronymy**, and just as we had co-hyponyms, the items in the list of car parts are **co-meronyms**. Other examples of meronymy include the parts of the human body (*arm, leg, neck, foot, hand,* etc.), the parts of a desktop computer (*screen, keyboard, mouse, hard drive, camera, USB port,* etc.), the rooms of a house, the parts of a tree, and so on. Murphy (2003: 231) says, 'Generally, meronymy is assumed to be a relation among names for things'. As with hyponymy, it is a noun-dominated category, where parts of entities can be organized as 'noun-like'/name concepts.

The linguist D. A. Cruse gives examples of other kinds of lexical relations ordered not by taxonomies or meronymy, but which are ways of sequencing items that do possess inherent relations of hierarchy or part-whole, etc. For example, *mountain, hill, mound,* and *hillock* are co-hyponyms of ELEVATED LAND which can also be ordered in terms of size, from small to big: *mound, hillock, hill, and mountain.* Similarly, *shoulder, upper arm, elbow, forearm, wrist,* and *hand,* as well as being co-meronyms as parts of the body, form a lexical chain in terms of one being attached to the other (Cruse 1986: 187–192).

MAKING SENSE IN THE REAL WORLD

Adrienne Lehrer has contributed greatly to our understanding of how we organize our worlds linguistically in relation to everyday life. In one of her many works on lexical fields, she provides an extensive taxonomy of verbs connected with cooking, but with the important addition of the nouns they collocate with (Lehrer 1969). Lehrer sees the organization of meaning within a lexical field not only in terms of co-hyponyms and superordinate words but also how they are differentiated by what people do in practice and through their knowledge of the world and the societies they inhabit. Lehrer takes a list of more than 30 cooking verbs (*fry, boil, poach, stew, braise,* etc.) and shows how complex their meanings are in relation to one another, for example, whether they employ water or fat, what types of utensils are involved, what type of heat is applied, what types of food are involved in each process, and so on. Thus, instead of just looking at individual words in lexical fields and how they relate to one another, Lehrer's analysis takes us into a 'universe of discourse' (Lehrer 1969: 54).

CORPUS EVIDENCE

The British National corpus (BNC1994) shows widely varying frequencies for some of the verbs Adrienne Lehrer lists in her study of cooking words. *Boil* and *bake* are many hundred times more common than *parboil* or *braise*. Other common terms are *fry* and *grill*. This may reflect the types of cooking British people typically engage in, telling us much about the real world and the 'universe of discourse', as well as the fact that some cooking terms are used figuratively (e.g., to *grill* somebody).

Elsewhere, Lehrer (1974: 95ff) shows how the same word can be used at different levels of generality for everyday convenience. Although the superordinate *cattle* is available, with *cow* being one of its hyponyms referring to an adult female, one will commonly hear people refer to 'the cows' in a field which might contain *calves, bullocks, heifers*, etc. *Cow*, for many people not involved in farming, is the **unmarked** (neutral) term that can be applied to cattle, while *heifer* would be a **marked** (more salient, specific) term. Lyons (1977: 308) gives a similar example in the case of *dog* and *bitch* and *sheep* and *ewe*. *Dog* can be both a superordinate applying to all dogs or a co-hyponym of *bitch*, contrasting male and female. In the sheep taxonomy, neither *ewe* nor *ram* has this double identity, so it is acceptable to ask, 'Is that a dog or a bitch?', but odd to ask, 'Is that a sheep or a ewe? *Dog* is an unmarked term, as is *duck* alongside the marked term *drake*.

The upside-down tree in Figure 3.4 was a taxonomy based on scientific characteristics of different types of fruit, an example of **strict** hyponymy. However, everyday groupings of words into 'families' can be far more loosely related. Cruse shows how people often organize words into *ad hoc* groupings that resemble hyponymy, but which are not taxonomic, so someone might say, 'the cupboard was full of books, vases, souvenirs and other junk' without entailing that if it is a *book*, it must be *junk*. Cruse calls this 'pseudo-hyponymy' (Cruse 1975). It is also called **lax** hyponymy. We will link this notion with a discussion of vague language in Chapter 6.

In another article, Cruse makes the point that how far up or down the hyponymy tree we choose the most appropriate word depends heavily on context and pragmatic meaning. If in my household we own one dog, a spaniel, I am likely to say, 'I'll just take the dog for a walk' rather than 'I'll just take the spaniel for a walk'. On the other hand, someone doing the rounds of a dog show and, wishing to know the breed of a dog standing with its owner, who asks the question 'What's that?' would be surprised and possibly irritated or feel patronized if the response was 'It's a dog' (Cruse 1977).

TAKING MEANING TO PIECES

PLUSES AND MINUSES TO EVERYTHING

Another approach to meaning compares words to one another in terms of their meaning components. For example, *cat* and *kitten* share a number of components: they are both animate, mammal, non-human, and feline, but they differ in terms of age, one being adult, the other not. These shared and non-shared components can be expressed using plus and minus signs, as in Table 3.1.

Breaking down words into their components of meaning in this way is called **componential analysis** (sometimes called **decomposition**), and the plus signs in Table 3.1 represent the **semantic components** of *cat* and *kitten*. Labels of the type +/− ANIMATE, +/− HUMAN, etc. were conceived of by anthropological linguists who founded the approach in the mid-twentieth century as 'a set of atomic components of lexical meaning that were assumed to be universal' (Lyons 1995: 106); in other words, componential analysis was able to tap into something all languages shared in terms of basic categories of experience. Componential analysis is a bit like the binary systems of a conventional computer: something either has or does not have a particular component as part of its meaning. All its components listed together define an entity, establish its place in a semantic field, and distinguish it from the other words in its lexical field.

Two famous names associated with this way of thinking were Jerrold Katz and Jerry Fodor, who published a paper in 1963 under the title *The Structure of a Semantic Theory*. In it, they laid out the

Table 3.1 Components of meaning: *cat* and *kitten*.

	Animate	Mammal	Human	Feline	Adult
cat	+	+	−	+	+
kitten	+	+	−	+	−

way words could be decomposed using **semantic markers** (e.g., *Human, Animal, Male*) and **distinguishers** (creating finer, idiosyncratic distinctions such as that between *bachelor* meaning 'unmarried man' and *bachelor* meaning 'holder of an academic degree'). Katz and Fodor state:

> The semantic markers and distinguishers are the means by which we can decompose the meaning of one sense of a lexical item into its atomic concepts, and thus exhibit the semantic structure IN a dictionary entry and the semantic relations BETWEEN dictionary entries.
>
> (Katz and Fodor 1963: 185–186 [their emphasis])

The markers were the most important feature of the semantic theory. 'Atomic concepts' is an apt metaphor for this way of breaking down words.

One problem with suggesting that componential analysis taps into universal aspects of experience is that the terms + HUMAN, + ADULT, being in our case expressed through English words, necessarily depend on the English meaning of those words (e.g., what constitutes 'adulthood'). Lyons adds an appropriate note of caution: 'This leaves open the obvious question: why should English, or any other natural language, have privileged status as a metalanguage for the semantic analysis of all languages?' (Lyons 1995: 109). Componential analysis tries to get round the problem by using a simple repertoire of basic, irreducible terms, called **semantic primes**, and usually writes them in a special font (e.g., capitals as we have done here) to indicate that they are not necessarily English words. As Murphy points out, the labels HUMAN, ADULT, etc. could be in any language and they would have the same status (Murphy 2010: 46).

However, it would be very laborious if we had to specify everything about a kitten from the fact that it is not a metal or a plant, all the way through the various divisions of animals, mammals, felines, and so on. For example, for most people, a *blueberry* does not need to be defined via all its scientific properties, all the way up the tree in Figure 3.4 and far beyond, as + BERRY + EDIBLE + SEEDS + FRUIT + PLANT − LOCOMOTIVE MOVEMENT + MULTICELLULAR ORGANISM, etc. *Blueberry* inherits all the primes without the need to state them explicitly. Our ability to automatically assume an entity's properties depends on what are called **redundancy rules**, which Murphy describes in this way:

> Redundancy rules reduce the number of components that need to be written in a semantic representation, as they guarantee that senses that have certain components will also be understood to have other components.

(Murphy 2010: 49)

However, a problem arises in componential analysis from the use of plus and minus signs: if *man* is + MALE and *woman* is + FEMALE, does it make any sense, logically or culturally, to say that *woman* is 'minus' MALE or that *man* is 'minus' FEMALE? The cultural aspect is by no means secondary, especially in societies where notions of gender and sex are widely debated, while, as already mentioned, notions such as 'adulthood' or 'old-agedness' take us further into culturally determined qualities.

Another problem with componential analysis is that it is not clear how wide its scope is in capturing the whole of the vocabulary. Examples such as *cat* and *kitten* are relatively straightforward, but what about words such as *angry, irate, furious, annoyed, irritated, peeved,* and *enraged*? Lyons suggests that when we look for components to list for any word, we use the most prototypical qualities to define them. The *Cambridge Dictionary Online*, for example, defines *irate* and *furious* in terms of degrees of being *angry*; the components of + ANGRY (negative emotion towards someone or something causing one to want to shout or challenge) are clearly seen as prototypical for the definition of the other words in the set, which are then defined as 'very angry', 'extremely angry', and so on. This again suggests that componential analysis is anything but objective or scientific and is heavily context- and culture-driven.

Can the use of plus and minus components meaningfully separate words in terms of their sense relations? Can we ever divorce from context the meanings of everyday words? For example, a simple term such as *children* can be − ADULT (*the children have to be at school by 8.30*) but could also in context be + ADULT. The question *Do you have any children?* addressed to a senior citizen might get the perfectly logical and culturally acceptable answer, *Yes, we have two and they're both married.* And let us not forget that the boundaries between terms in hyponymic systems are often somewhat vague and fuzzy. We considered the example of defining exactly what a vehicle was – what, therefore, would a reliable or objective componential analysis of *vehicle* look like? The core prototypical members of the VEHICLE category (cars, vans, buses) more readily supply the prime components of VEHICLE (+ MECHANICAL + LOCOMOTIVE MOVEMENT + TRANSPORTATION OF GOODS/PEOPLE) than marginal 'vehicles' such as snowmobiles or electric scooters.

Just how much complexity a componential analysis can involve is exemplified in Adrienne Lehrer's study of cooking terms which we looked at earlier, where she set out to chart the complexities of the 'universe of discourse' which everyday cooking takes us into. Lehrer refers to the usefulness of componential analysis but with this caveat:

> In a componential analysis one looks for the smallest number of components which will provide all of the relevant information, and so the most general elements are sought. However, some definitions call for quite specific and unique components, ...
>
> (Lehrer 1969: 46)

In the cooking study, Lehrer makes great use of the plus and minus signs to distinguish different cooking activities, though her distinctions do not claim to be semantic universals and for her, the binary nature of +/− is a mere convenience of labelling. The descriptions of meaning are rooted in activities familiar to her own culture. For instance, she defines the sense relation between *grill* and *fry* in this way:

> *Grill*: [-Liquid], [+Direct heat v. on griddle]
> or
> *Fry*: [-Liquid], [+Fat v. special utensil (frying pan)]
>
> (Lehrer 1969: 47)

Later, she devotes a whole page to a complex table of 35 different cooking verbs, using +/− notations to distinguish features of each one in terms of whether they use fat or other liquids, how vigorous the cooking is, how much time is involved, etc. but also what kinds of utensils are used and what the verbs collocate with. Lehrer's work is a componential analysis of the verbs involved in cooking, but it takes us a long way from the classical approach of seeking a small set of language universals.

Lyons (1995: 103) informs us that componential analysis was no longer as influential in the 1990s among linguistics as it had been in the previous decade, so perhaps we may dismiss it as a major preoccupation for the rest of this book. However, the classical model was influential in its time and is one among different ways of approaching meaning.

WORDS, THE MIND, AND THE WORLD

The story of componential analysis does not end with plus and minus signs and a somewhat limited set of semantic primes such as +/− HUMAN, however, and Murphy (2010: ch.4) considers how things have progressed to incorporate more conceptual approaches to meaning. In these perspectives, people and things are seen to interact with real-world events in a conceptually structured way, such that actions and events may be 'decomposed' into basic, universal notions of place, motion, thought, speech, etc. Meaning is thus more closely related to the concepts formed of the human mind. The study of this aspect of meaning is often called **conceptual semantics**. Conceptual semantics, says Singleton:

> ... essentially says that semantic structure exactly coincides with conceptual structure and that, therefore, any semantic analysis is also an analysis of mental representations.

> (Singleton 2016: 78)

The world, our experience of it, and our mental processing of it are manifested in the properties of the linguistic forms with which we word the world.

This basic introduction to semantics will go no further for the present, for another question underlies the study of meaning. The question is not just what words mean, but what speakers and writers mean by using words in different ways, in contexts, i.e., **pragmatic meaning**.

PRAGMATICS: WHAT DO *YOU* MEAN?

The field of **pragmatics** has grown in importance in recent decades as it attempts to illuminate what speakers intend to convey to their listeners rather than just what the words taken on their own mean. At this point, we can return to our earlier example from Cruse's discussion of the unexpected reply to the question by a visitor to a dog show curious to identify a breed, who asks of its owner, *What's that?* and gets the answer *It's a dog*. What is wrong here? The owner has answered truthfully and used the correct word to describe the canine mammal in question. But the owner has violated the **conversational maxims**. Conversational maxims, derived from the work of the linguistic philosopher Paul Grice (Grice 1975), are based around the **cooperative principle**, a set of unwritten rules as to how people behave cooperatively to communicate their meanings most effectively. Grice discussed four of these maxims, listed here with a brief gloss for each one:

1. Maxim of quantity (don't say too much or too little)
2. Maxim of quality (be truthful)
3. Maxim of relation (make your contribution relevant to the situation)
4. Maxim of manner (be clear; don't obfuscate or confuse)

It is clear that the dog owner who just says *It's a dog* is not giving enough information; the questioner wants to hear a word which is a hyponym of DOG, or, most probably, at a dog show, a hyponym of one of the common types of dogs, a hyponym of RETRIEVER, TERRIER, HOUND, etc., for example, *border terrier, golden retriever, American foxhound, cocker spaniel*, etc. Although truthful, the dog owner's reply is hardly relevant to the context and may be heard as sarcastic, patronising, or dismissive. Conversational maxims go a long way to explaining how and why speakers choose particular terms from the lexicon to suit the situation and how choices of words can change the reception of a message.

By no means can all of meaning, whether semantic or pragmatic, be analysed by just looking at individual words. We saw in Chapter 1 how combinations of words (compounds, phrasal verbs, and chunks of various kinds) were an integral feature of the lexicon, and at the end of this chapter we have briefly mentioned the interaction between words denoting people and things and words denoting activities, states, motion, etc. and how these relate to conceptual meaning categories. But we must also consider the fact that very often, we speak and write figuratively and exploit the language's repertoire of idiomatic expressions. We shall explore non-literal uses of vocabulary in Chapter 4.

FURTHER READING

Cruse, D. A. 1986 *Lexical Semantics*. Cambridge: Cambridge University Press.
This is a fairly advanced-level text covering all the important aspects of semantics. Cruse is known particularly for his work on hyponymy. The chapters on taxonomies and meronymy (Chapters 6 and 7) are relevant to the discussion of hyponymy in this chapter and take the subject further with detailed explanations and examples.

Murphy, M. L. 2010. *Lexical Meaning*. Cambridge: Cambridge University Press.
Murphy's chapters on componential analysis (Chapters 3 and 4) are clearly written, with many examples and further references to relevant literature. Her account of the developments from classical componential analysis to more cognitive approaches to meaning is especially useful.

Singleton, D. 2016. *Language and the Lexicon: An Introduction*. Abingdon, Oxon: Routledge.
Chapter 5 of Singleton's book covers the main types of sense relations (synonymy, antonymy, hyponymy, etc.) and also gives an excellent summary of cognitive approaches to meaning, including prototype theory.

4

BEATING ABOUT THE BUSH
FIGURATIVE MEANING

JUST IMAGINE

In Chapter 3, we considered words and their meanings in relation to when they can substitute for one another (synonymy), how oppositeness was based on shared properties (antonymy), and how words were related hierarchically or through part-whole and chain-like relationships (hyponymy and meronymy). At the heart of these statements of meaning is the idea that we humans organize and categorize our experience and perceive similarities and differences in the world around us and what happens in it. On the one hand, we see words as labels for interrelated entities and processes in the world but on the other hand, it is also apparent that words enable us to mould our experience creatively, to enable us to understand and compare entities and processes by speaking of them imaginatively, that is to say we can use words and expressions figuratively.

Figurative meaning is usually contrasted with **basic** or **literal** meaning. On the face of it, this seems straightforward, and we usually know when someone is speaking 'figuratively' and when their remarks should not be taken literally. However, it would be wrong to think of literal meaning in terms of a straight-line, one-to-one relationship between a word and some entity or process in the world, a point we made at the start of Chapter 3. David Ritchie, in his introduction to the study of metaphors says, '*Literal* ordinarily implies a code-like one-to-one *mapping* of words with meanings. Very few words afford such a direct mapping' (Ritchie 2013: 10). He instead proposes a continuum from literal to figurative, with areas in between.

DOI: 10.4324/9781003284611-5

Linguists have long discussed the problems associated with assigning 'literal' meanings to words and expressions. Mira Ariel, for example, argues that literal meaning may correspond to the most salient meaning of the word – the meaning that is uppermost in our minds, or to the meaning that tallies with a relevant contribution to a discourse (Ariel 2002). Salient meaning is an important psycholinguistic reflex which triggers a literal interpretation. Rachel Giora sees it as the most prominent meaning we hold in our mental lexicon thanks to the frequency of that meaning and our familiarity with it (Giora 1999). The **mental lexicon**, the vocabulary store we hold in our minds, is a theme which we shall return to in Chapter 5. Nonetheless, it is generally accepted that a great deal of our everyday language is figurative in some way, in that we are naturally inclined as humans to see analogies between different types of experience and to exploit them as a way of organizing our worlds.

ATOMS OR MOLECULES?

In Chapter 3, most of the discussion centred around the meanings of words and how they may be represented in terms of their denotation (their meanings in the world) and their relationships with other words (sense relations). However, meaning cannot fully be understood just by examining single words. In Chapter 1, we mentioned how words come together in the form of compounds, phrasal verbs, and other multi-word expressions or chunks. The existence of different types of recurrent word combinations has significant implications for understanding how we create and decode meaning, especially in relation to the question of non-literal and idiomatic meaning.

If we ask a computer to search a corpus and tell us how often the same combination of two or three or four or five words occur, we will very quickly see how some multi-word strings are very common indeed. Take for example the six-word string *at the end of the day*. It occurs 760 times in the BNC 1994; in that respect, it is more than 200 times more frequent than *inquire, autobiography, blackmail, cocoa, nostalgia, wasp,* and *cookery* – none of which would be considered obscure words in British English present-day usage. What is more, *at the end of the day* more often than not has a meaning other than 'when the sun sets' or 'the hour before midnight' or any other reference to the clock. In other words, literal meaning (the salient, denotative meaning of each word taken one by one) does not supply the meaning intended by its users. Its most common use is figurative, that is to say *end* and *day* are used to represent a situation analogous to the 23rd hour of the clock, in this case the 'final stage of a process'. Its figurative meaning is thus commonly heard as 'in the end' or 'when all things are considered'.

CORPUS EVIDENCE

Here are some typical examples of speakers using *at the end of the day* in the BNC 1994.

Well at the end of the day all our work is for the benefit of children, individual children, individual human beings like you or like me. (JNG)
There's no such thing as failure, at the end of the day there's only results. (JND)
But at the end of the day, there simply is no point in punishing criminals if you can't catch them. (JS9)

But do we derive the figurative meaning of strings like *at the end of the day* by decoding the individual words? Dwight Bolinger, in a critique of the semantic theory of Katz and Fodor which we mentioned when discussing componential analysis in Chapter 3, examines the expression *a spell of warm weather*, where *spell*, taken alone and out of context, is ambiguous between 'period of time' and 'act of enchantment'. He rejects the idea that it is the words *of weather* which disambiguate the two meanings:

> Or we can say, as I would say, there was no ambiguity to begin with: that *spell of weather* is a previously learned unit in the same way that *pretend* is a previously learned unit, and that *of weather* no more disambiguates *spell* than *pre-* disambiguates *tend* by excluding the meaning 'to have a tendency'.
>
> (Bolinger 1965: 571)

Bolinger was writing in the pre-corpus era, but corpus evidence has only served to add weight to his claim that previously learned units are processed as wholes – 'previously learned' need not be taken to mean consciously learned but rather the result of the language user's continuous exposure to the language, and the frequency of the expression. Katz and Fodor (1963: 186) had referred to the decomposition of a lexical item into its 'atomic concepts'. Bolinger's 1965 critique is appropriately titled *The Atomization of Meaning*. Decomposing words as we might decompose chemicals into molecules and atoms becomes a mechanistic operation, a basic programme for a very basic computer that discards so much of the complexity of how we experience the world and how we encode and decode acts of communication.

BITE-SIZED CHUNKS

The expression *at the end of the day* displays fixedness in that we do not find speakers saying *at the finish of the day* or *when the day has ended* without sounding odd or without changing the meaning in some way and losing the figurative meaning. We must therefore take into account two important features when we examine multi-word units (MWUs):

- Degree of fixedness – can the words in the MWU be changed or rearranged in any way?
- Degree of figurative meaning – is the MWU commonly used both literally and figuratively, or just one way or the other?

Much has been written about the frequency of recurring sequences of words in corpus data, and numerous different names have been given to the strings of words that constantly recur, including *clusters, chunks, n-grams, phrasal expressions, fixed expressions, formulaic language, lexical bundles, frozen formulae,* and *formulaic sequences* (e.g., Wray 2000; Schmitt 2004; Biber 2009; Martinez and Schmitt 2012). In this book, for convenience's sake, we shall refer to MWUs as chunks.

Some common chunks are so frequent in everyday conversation that we hardly notice them. In the Spoken BNC2014, *you know* is by far the most frequent combination of two words, occurring more than 45,000 times in the 11.5 million words of the corpus; it also stands at number one in the list of two-word chunks occurring in the Spoken Open American National Corpus (SOANC). Some of its occurrences are literal, referring to knowledge of or acquaintance with someone or something, as in this example:

*Do **you know** that film 'Metropolis'?* (Spoken BNC2014 S263)

Other occurrences, more than 1,000, are part of the longer chunks *you know what I mean* and *do you know what I mean*. These can be seen in this example:

*That is really tasty it doesn't taste like risotto rice it tastes more like basmati **do you know what I mean?*** (Spoken BNC2014 S2DD)

Then there are cases where *you know* is used to launch a conversational topic, a way of saying, 'I'm sure you're familiar with what I'm going to talk about', as here:

*Hey **you know** that book? erm The Curious Incident of the Dog in the Night-Time ... that title has come from Sherlock Holmes Hound of the Baskervilles* (Spoken BNC2014 S3AC)

However, *you know* seems overwhelmingly to mean 'I'm assuming you and I are on the same wavelength, and I don't need to explain or justify what I'm saying'. *You know* has become a fixed formula for this figurative, idiomatic meaning in conversation. In a random sample of 100 occurrences in the Spoken BNC 2014, no fewer than 91 show *you know* used in the way seen in these examples:

*He's going through a divorce at the moment and eh **you know** as friends you want to sort of be there* (Spoken BNC2014 S4L9)
*I don't know anything about houses **you know** I'm a complete novice* (Spoken BNC2014 SUUE)

Another high-frequency chunk is *I mean*, which occurs almost 20,000 times in the Spoken BNC2014. A study of *you know* and *I mean*, by Fox Tree and Schrock (2002), investigated how the basic conversational functions of the two expressions relate to the speaker inviting the listener to make appropriate inferences (*you know*) and signalling to the listener that some adjustment to the message is happening (*I mean*). In both cases, the meanings can be seen as fig- urative extensions of core meanings of the verbs *to know* and *to mean*. However, most speakers would not think of the expressions as 'figurative' since they are so common, banal and subliminal, a fact which is true of many everyday chunks. The main point is that *you know* typically acts like a single word, a single item in the lexicon, in the same way that *I mean* and *at the end of the day* typically act as units. Thus, meaning in the lexicon must be seen as consisting of the semantics of all its single words plus the semantics of the many compound forms and chunks that encode unitary meanings.

The linguist John Sinclair, who was a pioneer in corpus research, put forward what he called **the idiom principle**, based on his observations of corpus data. Sinclair and his team set out to write what was an innovative dictionary based on real usage in a large corpus (Sinclair 1987). It soon became apparent, however, that conventional, word-by-word definitions simply did not cover the meanings that could be read in the corpus data and that a large pro- portion of language production and the creation of meaning was achieved through the use of chunks. Sinclair concluded from his corpus analyses that:

> A language user has available to him or her a large number of semi- preconstructed phrases that constitute single choices, even though they might appear to be analysable into segments.
>
> (Sinclair, 1991: 110)

ROOM FOR MANOEUVRE

Chunks are not always completely fixed as continuous strings; their unitary meaning may still be observed in **discontinuous chunks**. For example, in the written texts of the BNC 1994, there are just over 1,000 examples of the string *as far as x (be) concerned*, where x represents anything from one to nine words. Table 4.1 shows the most common patterns.

The intervening string may be quite long, for example, *as far as early childhood educational opportunities are concerned*, *as far as simplicity and accord with observations of planetary positions are concerned* and *as far as receiving knowledge relating to undertakings of fitness for purpose is concerned*. Despite these long intervening strings, the unitary meaning

Table 4.1 Discontinuous chunk: *As far as [...] (be) concerned.*

Corpus Example	Pattern
as far as [proper noun] *is/was/were concerned*	*as far as Alice was concerned*
as far as [common noun] *is/was concerned*	*as far as aromatherapy is concerned*
as far as [personal pronoun] *is/was concerned*	*as far as I am concerned*

of *as far as x (be) concerned,* as a way of specifying or drawing attention to a person or thing, remains intact.

Other chunks offer less flexibility. The string *the turn of the century* normally only allows numbers (e.g., *twentieth, nineteenth*) or adjectives (*last, present*) to intervene between *the* and *century*. The expression *on the spur of the moment,* meaning to decide or to act quickly without planning, seems to allow nothing to intervene in the chunk. Discontinuous chunks often have preferred patterns, even though there may be various options. The string *the tip of ... iceberg* (meaning the smallest part of a problem while the largest part is hidden) allows *the* or *an* to fill the gap, but *the* is many times more frequent (Figure 4.1). And of the words preceding the chunk, the adverbs *only, just,* and *merely*, in descending order, are the most common.

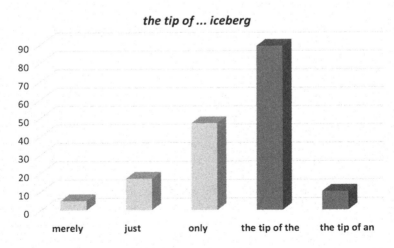

the tip of ... iceberg

Figure 4.1 The tip of the iceberg.

In her ground-breaking corpus-based study of idioms, Rosamund Moon lists variation in the forms of idioms where, for example, a verb may change (*lower/drop one's guard*), or a noun (*burn one's boats/bridges*), along with examples of substitution of other word classes (Moon 1998: 124–152). Cronk and Schweigert (1992) also give examples of idioms which show variability of form to a greater or lesser degree.

AS CLEAR AS MUD: IDIOMS

Although they are used figuratively, expressions such as *at the end of the day* and *the tip of the iceberg* are not too difficult to decipher in context, especially if we have sufficient knowledge of the world (encyclopaedic knowledge) that tells us that the activities of the day typically have some sort of conclusion, and that most of an iceberg is submerged and invisible. Their meanings are, relatively speaking, **transparent**. Decoding would take place 'via normal linguistic processing, augmented by minimal inferences' (Cacciari and Glucksberg 1995: 286), and besides, for most speakers the chunks are familiar because of their frequency. Other fairly transparent chunks include *were it not for the fact that*, and *to get to the bottom of (a question/an issue)*. At the other end of the scale are quite opaque idioms such as *to buy a pig in a poke, cloud cuckoo land,* and *to have a bee in one's bonnet*. **Idioms** are expressions that are peculiar to a language; they are often unpredictable and **opaque** (their meaning is not obvious from the individual words that make them up).

The *Cambridge Idioms Dictionary* (2006) contains some 7,000 idiomatic expressions used in British, American, and Australian English, based on corpus evidence. The idioms were chosen as being the most useful for learners of English as a second or foreign language, but there are many hundreds of idiomatic expressions in use in English around the world that did not make the dictionary. Idioms come in various shapes and sizes. Table 4.2 shows examples of different types.

Idioms are generally colourful and salient, standing out from more neutral uses of vocabulary in any text or conversation. Some are fun to use because of their sound patterns, for example, rhyming compounds such as *nitty-gritty, hurly-burly,* and *higgledy-piggledy*, or

Table 4.2 Types of idioms.

Type	Characteristics	Example
Tournure idiom	Usually a clause with a verb and object	*break the ice; spill the beans; make a mountain out of a molehill*
Phrasal verb idiom	A verb and particle with opaque meaning	*take over (assume authority, responsibility); drop off (fall asleep), own up (confess)*
Irreversible binomials and trinomials	Two/three items of the same word class connected by *and* (sometimes *or*), always in the same sequence	*doom and gloom, part and parcel, back and forth, win or lose, lock, stock and barrel, cool, calm and collected*
Idiomatic simile or comparison	An adjective and a noun connected by *as ... as ...*, or expressions with *like ...*	*as long as your arm, as cool as a cucumber, as red as a beetroot, like clockwork, like a bat out of hell*
Idiomatic phrase	A phrase with idiomatic meaning	*a flash in the pan, out for the count, famous last words, up for grabs*
Idiomatic compound	Two or more words forming a compound with an idiomatic meaning	*hanger-on, earth-shattering, brain drain, bone-dry, tongue-twister, happy-go-lucky, hurly-burly, sabre-rattling*

ablaut compounds, for example, *chit-chat, mishmash,* and *flip-flop* (see the discussion of these types in Chapter 1).

DO YOU SEE WHAT I MEAN?

One question we can ask about idioms is: do the literal meanings of their component words contribute to how we decode them? If someone says *I was over the moon when I heard the news,* we do not assume that they were an astronaut travelling in a spaceship. That would be a literal interpretation of their words. But if we say someone *is skating on thin ice,* do we immediately picture a person on ice-skates moving across dangerously thin ice? Or do we not think of ice at all and simply immediately access the typical contextual meaning of 'doing something dangerous or risky'? Raymond Gibbs, who has published a number of studies investigating how people process idioms, suggests that conventional uses of idioms (that is to say in their most typical, figurative uses) are more quickly and directly accessed than literal interpretations. Gibbs says, in discussing the results of his experiments:

> These data argue against a serial process model of nonliteral language processing, in which the literal meaning of an utterance is first determined, before the conveyed interpretation is derived.
>
> (Gibbs 1980: 155)

In a later article reiterating this point, Gibbs adds: 'This does not mean that people never examine the conventional meanings of the individual words in idiomatic expressions' (Gibbs 1986: 28). The degree to which visualization of literal meaning might occur is likely to depend on the type of idiom. I recently heard a commentator on a BBC World Service radio broadcast promising to 'join the dots' in relation to a particular news story. In my mind, this immediately triggered a memory of an activity which was common in puzzle-books when I was a child – you joined a series of dots on a page to make a picture of an object or an animal, for example. This memory matches well with the dictionary definition of *join the dots* as 'to make connections between people or events that seem not to be connected so that you can understand what is happening' (*Macmillan Dictionary Online*).[1] It is likely that the power of visualization also depends on the degree of abstractness of an idiom, with more abstract idioms being less prone to visualization; it is difficult to conjure up an immediately meaningful image of *nitty-gritty* (meaning 'the basics') or an idiomatic phrasal verb such as *to put one over on somebody* (meaning to deceive them) compared with more concrete expressions such as *to throw a spanner in the works* or *light at the end of the tunnel*. In other words, the literal, word-by-word meaning may sometimes be more helpful than others.

The literal meanings of some idiomatic expressions may have become opaque over time such that they give little or no clue as to the idiomatic interpretation – one either knows the idiom or one does not: *to buy a pig in a poke, to kick the bucket,* and *to kick over the traces* all have somewhat obscure origins in rural/agricultural practices and give few clues to their idiomatic meaning. Context usually helps with decoding, and we mostly only ever encounter language in context: *He does a great take-off of Donald Trump* is not likely to be confused with *seat belts must be kept securely fastened during take-off and landing.*

Gibbs sums up the situation succinctly: 'Speakers and hearers know the meanings of many conventional, formulaic utterances and appear to comprehend their nonliteral meanings immediately, even if their literal interpretations do not make sense' (Gibbs 1986: 28). Idioms, like other MWUs, are just like long words, albeit they are written with spaces within them at conventional word-boundaries.

REFLECTION POINT

What visual images, if any, do these idiomatic expressions trigger in your mind?

hoity-toity   *toe the line*   *push the boat out*   *by hook or by crook*
pocket money

IN A NUTSHELL

In 1998, I published a book about spoken English and included a chapter on idioms. My concern arose from the fact that materials for teaching English as a second language often treated idioms and other figurative expressions merely as a form of entertainment in the vocabulary lesson. I was interested to see how people used them in everyday conversation and why they should choose them over and above literal expressions. I concluded that idioms were not just colourful and informal alternatives to their literal equivalents and that they were particularly useful as summaries and evaluations of situations (McCarthy 1998: 131–149). Idioms and similar figurative expressions are community 'badges of membership' and can be used to project to one's listeners a common bond of understanding and empathy. They are able to summarize shared feelings and perspectives; in other words, they can express ideas *in a nutshell* – itself a good example of what idioms can do. In these examples from the Spoken BNC2014, idiomatic expressions are bolded; they show speakers using them to evaluate and sum up situations, repeating and rewording one another's vocabulary to show convergence and understanding:

[Speaker 0308 is talking about a university]

<S0308> *so I trained there I did my degree there I did my masters there and then I finished up lecturing there*
<S0266> **fully circle**
<S0308> *yeah* **full circle** *and my colleague there he went to college the same time that you did, seventy to seventy-three*
<S0266> *oh right*
<S0308> *mm*
<S0266> *mm*
<S0308> **small world**
<S0266> **small world**
<S0268> **what goes around comes around**

(SBFN)

<S0446"> *the north side* <pause> *up on the north side* <pause> *the beaches there are absolutely amazing*
<S0352 " > *but the scenery* <pause > *is lacking*
<S0446> *is* <pause> *yeah* <pause> *it's* **flat as a pancake**
<S0329> *there's no trees?*
<S0352> *there's no, any not a tree on it*

(S6JP)

IDIOM-PRONE

Some aspects of our experience tend to be the source of a large number of idiomatic expressions; they are **idiom-prone**. Physical movement is a powerful source of figurative expressions: we can *take steps to achieve a goal, walk away from a problem, go with the flow, run into difficulties, jump to a conclusion, go the extra mile, sidestep an issue, enter uncharted territory, make a beeline for something*, and so on. In Chapter 3, we mentioned the parts of the human body as an example of the relationship of meronymy. Since the human body is such a central element of our experience, it is not surprising that its meronyms are idiom-prone. We *head for* places, *thumb a lift, elbow*

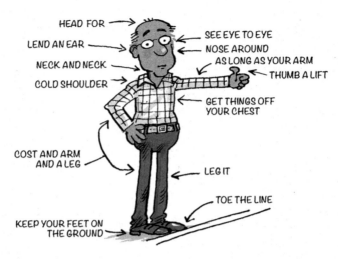

Figure 4.2 Body-part idioms. Image © Jake Tebbit 2022.

our way through somewhere, *get things off our chest, take something to* heart, and so on.

Figure 4.2 shows examples of body-based idioms. Some are more directly aligned with physical action (e.g., *thumb a lift, hand something over*); others are more metaphorical (e.g., *nose around, give somebody the cold shoulder*). Moon (1998: 184–185) discusses the tension between literal and figurative interpretations of body-part expressions. Meanwhile, a study based on a dictionary analysis of English, German, Swedish, Russian, and Finnish body-part idioms found that the hand, the head, and the eye were the three most idiom-prone sources in the languages examined (Niemi et al. 2013).

REFLECTION POINT

The idioms in Figure 4.2 are by no means a complete list of idioms connected with the human body, and you may be able to add more from your own vocabulary or ones which you have encountered in other languages you may know.

Oher idiom-prone entities are based on animals: domestic, farm, and wild animals all provide rich material for metaphors and idioms. Here are some examples:

Domestic: *like the cat that ate the cream, a hang-dog expression, barking up the wrong tree*
Farm: *chicken out, a load of bull, to milk something, to rule the roost, pecking order*
Wild: *a wolf in sheep's clothing, a sly old fox, the lion's share, the elephant in the room*

Food and drink, too, provide a fertile source domain for idioms, as in Table 4.3.

The question of whether the sources of idioms are universal is difficult to demonstrate, but there certainly seem to be commonalities across languages, as we saw in the body-part examples. Swedish shares a number of animal idioms with English, for example, *fri som en fågel (free as a bird), envis som en åsna (stubborn as a mule), glad som en lärka (happy as a lark)*, and *hal som en ål (slippery as an eel)*. The Spanish idiom *coger el toro por los cuernos* translates directly to English as *take the bull by the horns,* while other idioms vary to different degrees as between English and Spanish, for example, Spanish *más loco que una cabra* ('crazier than a goat') matches English *as mad as a hatter/a March hare.* For further variations between English and Spanish in idioms connected with the notion of 'craziness', see Corpas Pastor (2021). Boers and Stengers (2008) also compare Spanish and English idioms and list a number of shared sources for idioms between the two languages, for example, vehicles, sports, entertainment, cooking, religion, and superstition. Where this is a correspondence of meaning between idioms in two languages, the extent to which the wording is similar is referred to as the degree of **congruency**.

Table 4.3 Food- and drink-based expressions.

make a meal of sth	*small fry*
chew over sth	*butter sb up*
a cocktail (of toxic chemicals)	*the breadwinner*
leave a bitter taste	*want jam on it*
sth is baked into sth	*pie in the sky*
wine and dine	*bring home the bacon*
be full of beans	*the icing on the cake*

The examples of English idioms cited so far in this chapter are all ones which speakers of British English should be familiar with. Many such idioms will also be familiar to speakers of other varieties of English. In a study of idioms in Nigerian English, Aliyu Muhammad Umar not only finds commonalities with British English idioms but also discusses uniquely Nigerian idioms with their roots in indigenous languages, concluding, concerning Nigerian English in general: 'This variety has helped Nigerians to express their world-view in an international medium of communication like the English language' (Umar 2019: 30). This statement underlies the strong cultural element in idioms.

Elisabeth Piirainen, in a paper examining the question whether the apparent recent spread of the same or similar idioms geographically across different languages can be put down to globalization and Anglo-American influences, shows that many of the common idioms in European languages have a long pedigree and can be traced back to biblical or classical sources or fables and many are hundreds of years old. She concludes that the historical and cultural roots of idioms shared across European languages are more significant than any supposed recent Anglo-American influence and global linguistic domination (Piirainen 2010). Idioms run deep in the cultural makeup of communities and are by no means frivolous extras in the lexicons of languages (see also Piirainen 2005).

LOOK AT IT THIS WAY

METAPHORS

One way of looking at idiomatic meaning is that idioms may be associated with **conceptual metaphors**. Conceptual metaphors are basic ways of creating analogies among entities and processes in the world – we understand one thing or idea in terms of another. An example would be COMMUNICATION IS COMMERCE, where expressions such as *sell an idea, peddle a lie, buy what someone says, trade insults*, and *set out one's stall* are compared with buying and selling goods and services. Conceptual metaphors are most associated with the work of the cognitive linguists George Lakoff and Mark Johnson in the book *Metaphors We Live By* (Lakoff and

Johnson 1980/2003). The opening words of the book lay out their central premise:

> Metaphor is for most people a device of the poetic imagination and the rhetorical flourish—a matter of extraordinary rather than ordinary language. Moreover, metaphor is typically viewed as characteristic of language alone, a matter of words rather than thought or action. For this reason, most people think they can get along perfectly well without metaphor. We have found, on the contrary, that metaphor is pervasive in everyday life, not just in language but in thought and action. Our ordinary conceptual system, in terms of which we both think and act, is fundamentally metaphorical in nature.
>
> (Lakoff and Johnson 1980/2003: 3)

Raymond Gibbs links the idea of conceptual metaphors to the meanings of idioms, even idioms which seem to be 'dead' metaphors, i.e., idioms which once upon a time were clear metaphors but which have lost their metaphorical power over time. He claims:

> ... idioms have complex figurative interpretations that are not arbitrarily determined but are motivated by independently existing conceptual metaphors that provide the foundation for much of our everyday thought and reasoning.
>
> (Gibbs 1992: 485–486)

Conceptual metaphors such as THE MIND IS A CONTAINER help explain the figurative meaning of expressions such as *spill the beans, let the cat out of the bag, think outside the box, to be empty-headed, to put an idea into someone's head*, etc. Metaphors work through activating a **source domain** (e.g., the mind as a box, bag or other container) which is mapped onto a **target domain** (e.g., *the beans* and *the cat* are things that spill or jump out of an opened container, they are 'secrets carelessly revealed'). However, the extent to which such powerful metaphors play a part in idiom processing is open to question. Cacciari and Glucksberg (1995) in a series of experiments testing the effects of accessing literal meanings in relation to idiomatic meanings concluded that 'visual imagery does not provide convincing evidence for the role of conceptual metaphors in idiom comprehension' (p. 303).

INFORMATION ADD-ON

A number of expressions are based around the notion of warfare and armed conflict:

bombard someone with questions   beat a retreat   a ticking time-bomb
to take aim at someone   to keep one's powder dry   a silver bullet
to torpedo a suggestion/an idea   to be gunning for someone
to hold a pistol to someone's head   to be shot down in flames

PROVERBS AND METAPHORS

Proverbs and sayings around the world seem to respond to a deep human instinct to make sense of life and our experiences. They are effectively 'long lexical chunks' which pack in a lot of meaning. Like other chunks, their form is usually fixed. They are based on metaphors in the sense of their being characterized by source and target domains. They are, by their very nature, general statements which are applied to particular situations – the GENERIC and the SPECIFIC, respectively, as Gibbs et al. (1996) call the conceptual-metaphorical framework or schema of proverbs. A proverb such as *Don't count your chickens before they hatch* is a generic statement that can be applied in a specific situation where someone is anticipating a positive future and ignoring the possibility that things may turn out to be not as hoped. The metaphorical basis of the proverb can be seen as EVENTS ARE BIRTHS – the events are the gestating future; the births are hatched eggs. Just as with other idiomatic fixed expressions, the listener immediately accesses the figurative meaning, and chickens and eggs hatching, in the literal sense probably play little or no part in comprehension.

REFLECTION POINT

Here are some well-known English proverbs. Consider how may more you can add from your own variety of English and whether you ever use them yourself. If you know other languages, are there similar proverbs in those languages?

> *Every cloud has a silver lining*
> *The machine that squeaks the loudest gets the oil*
> *Look before you leap*
> *A bird in the hand is worth two in the bush*

The *Routledge Book of World Proverbs* (Stone 2006) contains more than 16,000 proverbs and sayings from all over the world and shows how the kinds of messages they convey transcend languages, cultures, and nations, with common themes existing across different communities.

INFORMATION ADD-ON

Here are some examples of proverbs in other languages and their nearest equivalents in English.

Spanish: *El que mucho abarca poco aprieta – Don't bite off more than you can chew*

Swedish: *Allt är inte guld som glimmer – All that glitters is not gold*

Japanese: *Kōryō kui ari – Pride goes before a fall* (source: Buchanan 1965: 9)

French: *À cheval donné on ne regarde pas les dents – Don't look a gift horse in the mouth*

Welsh: *Carreg a dreigla, ni fwsoga – A rolling stone gathers no moss*

Bahasa Malaysia: *Tong kosong nyaring bunyinya – An empty vessel makes the most noise*

TROPES GALORE

HERE COMES THE ARMY: METONYMY

We shall now consider further aspects of figurative uses of vocabulary under the general heading of **tropes**, i.e., frequently used figures of speech. We start with metonymy. **Metonymy** comes about when one aspect or one entity or part of something is used to represent the whole entity. Jeannette Littlemore, in her book on metonymy, offers this definition:

> Metonymy is a cognitive and linguistic process through which we use one thing to refer to another. For example, we might use the word 'Hollywood' to refer to mainstream American films, or the word 'Shakespeare' to refer to plays and poetry by Shakespeare. In these examples, a place and a person are used to refer to things that are strongly related to that particular place and that particular person.
>
> (Littlemore 2015: 1)

Someone who sees one soldier arriving on the scene might say 'Here comes the army', where a single soldier is seen as a symbol of the whole military force of which the soldier is a member. Or someone might say 'The hospital sent her home after just two days' – it was a medical practitioner, not the hospital building or whole institution which made the decision to discharge the patient. *The army* and *the hospital* are used metonymically. Other examples British and American readers will be familiar with are *Downing Street* and *The White House*, which are often used by the news media to refer to the whole central apparatus of the UK and US governments, respectively (e.g., *Downing Street refused to comment, The White House issued a statement*). British readers will also be familiar with reports such as *Buckingham Palace has released a statement* to refer to official communications emanating from the monarch's office, or *Number ten has denied the allegations* (reference to the UK Prime Minister's official residence at 10 Downing Street, London).

We don't see or hear these examples as extraordinary, humorous, visually impactful, or colourful in the way that idioms such as *cut off the hand that feeds you* or *walk a tightrope* might be received. Metonyms are typically unmarked, i.e., heard as normal, neutral, not standing out, though unconventional, marked metonymy is always available to creative users of the language such as poets, humourists, advertisers, and journalists.

Metonymy is different from metaphor; metaphor is based on a source domain and a target domain, as we have noted. Recall the example of THE MIND IS A CONTAINER, where the 'box' or 'bag' of the mind (the source) is seen as spilling out its contents inadvertently when someone 'lets the cat out of the bag' or 'spills the beans' (the target: 'reveals a secret'). In metonymy, there are not conceptually separate source and target domains: the solider is a member of the army, the White House is where the President of the USA lives and works, and so on. *Soldier* and *army*, and *White House* and *President* are related terms; *the mind* and *a bag* are not – they are brought together in the making of a conceptual metaphor.

Littlemore is interested in how metonymy works in real-world, everyday communication, not just as a cognitive-linguistic category. She concludes:

> When we look at metonymy in this way, we can see that it has a number of characteristics that show it to be a far more interesting and unpredictable phenomenon than one might think. Taken together, these characteristics show that metonymy works just as hard as metaphor and that it does just as many things as metaphor.
>
> (Littlemore 2015: 191)

The word *metaphor* will be quite familiar to many non-specialists, but the term *metonymy* has always been a specialized piece of terminology. This is reflected in their relative frequencies in the BNC1994: *metaphor(s)/metaphoric(ally)* display 1,300 occurrences, while *metonymy/metonyms/metonymous/metonymic(ally)* have fewer than 20 occurrences. However, debate continues as to the precise difference, if any, between metaphor and metonymy. Jeannette

CORPUS EVIDENCE

In a random sample of 100 occurrences of the word *Hollywood* in the BNC 1994 Informative Texts segment, only seven are literal references to an actual geographical location (e.g., *Brad Pitt's ageing West Hollywood bungalow*), while more than 90% are metonymic references to the film industry, its clusters of famous studios, and the stars who populate the movie industry scene, for example:

Hollywood legend Audrey Hepburn, Hollywood's golden age, Hollywood's portrayal of Vietnam, Hollywood heart-throb, Hollywood stardom

Right-hand collocates with a frequency greater than 10 in the 1,501 occurrences of *Hollywood* in the BNC 1994 Informative dataset are shown in the graph (Figure 4.3).

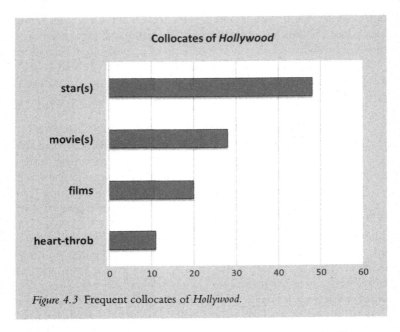

Figure 4.3 Frequent collocates of *Hollywood*.

Littlemore, as we have seen, views metonymy as pervading our everyday communication. Another corpus linguist, Alice Deignan, prefers to view many of the instances of conceptual metaphor cited in the literature as metonyms and argues:

> To see them now as metonymous rather than metaphorical raises the question of whether metonymy should be regarded as a more central trope than metaphor.

(Deignan 2005a: 72)

In her book of the same year, Deignan takes the discussion of metaphor and metonymy into further detail (Deignan 2005b). We have discussed idiomatic expressions associated with the human body (Figure 4.1). Are idioms such as *toe the line* or *see eye to eye* based on conceptual metaphors with the human body-parts as their source domain, or is the *toe* a metonym for a whole person behaving correctly by *toeing the line*, just as *eye*[1] and *eye*[2] are metonyms for two whole people when they *see eye to eye*? Rosamund Moon, in her

book on fixed expressions and idioms (what she calls FEIs), high-
lights the role that body-parts play in metonymy and notes:

> The particular body part represents the whole person, as well as fore-
> grounding the physical sense or ability which constitutes the central part
> of the FEI's meaning.

(Moon 1998: 194)

Metonymy and metaphor are best seen as interacting and are rather
based on a scale or cline, with 'more metaphoric' at one end and
'more metonymic' at the other. Deignan (2005a) has a table repre-
senting the scale, with examples at each end and various types of
overlap in between. Metonymy, it would seem then, is not an
obscure, fringe category of vocabulary and meaning, but is a very
basic way of structuring figurative meaning and making sense of our
environment and experiences, both physical and social.

NO EXAGGERATION: HYPERBOLE

Sometimes, vocabulary is used to describe people and things in a
way which we know cannot be true, since the speaker or writer is
exaggerating beyond plausible reality. The speaker who says 'I've
got millions of cousins' is engaging in **hyperbole**. When people
use hyperbole, they do not mean to be taken literally, and we usually know, based on our knowledge of the world or of the context,
when someone is exaggerating.

My late colleague Ronald Carter and I investigated hyperbole
in a spoken English corpus and found that certain types of vocabulary were prone to hyperbolic use (McCarthy and Carter 2004).
Numbers and quantities and measures of time and distance are a
case in point, with expressions such as *dozens of, hundreds/thou-
sand/millions of* often being used counter factually to intensify a
statement or to create humour. Similarly, *mountains of food, tons of
rubbish* in one's waste bin, *heaps of money,* and so on. We know that
uses of these expressions often cannot be true (people do not literally have *millions of cousins*) but we normally do not accuse them of
lying; we are more likely to just smile or at most to say 'don't
exaggerate'.

Exaggeration can go in two broad directions: expanding the magnitude of something or, in the other direction, shrinking its magnitude. So, a house bigger than the norm in a given context might be described as *enormous*, *ginormous*, or *massive*, while a house smaller than the norm might be described as *tiny*, *teeny-weeny*, or *poky*. The scientist who said, 'space is so extraordinarily vast' (*New Scientist* magazine 15 January 2022: 12) is heard as making a literal statement about the almost incomprehensible size of the universe. Someone who says 'Joe's front garden is so extraordinarily vast' is likely to be heard as exaggerating. A nearby shop may be dismissed as *miles away* if someone is too lazy to walk to it, or *you just have to fall out of bed* if we want to persuade someone that they have a convenient shop nearby.

Often, exaggeration is used for emotive intensification: Colston and O'Brien (2000a: 180) give the example of 'very negative comments made about moderately negative situations', which we might witness in someone saying, 'This is the world's worst restaurant' or 'You'd wait forever for a bus here'. Kreuz and Roberts (1995) investigated the relationship between hyperbole and irony: an ironic tone of voice may be accompanied by overstatement with comments such as 'Isn't that just wonderful!' to describe a bad event or situation. Hyperbole may also be achieved through repetition of words or combinations of hyperbolic terms, e.g., *millions and millions of, hundreds and thousands of, loads and loads of,* any of which can be applied counterfactually to small or relatively neutral/normal numbers and amounts of people and things.

John Barnden, an artificial intelligence expert, notes a kind of reflexive hyperbole in statements such as 'Sailing isn't just a part of Mike's life, it is his life' (Barnden 2018: 219), where we can see an overlap with metonymy (sailing becomes a symbol of the whole, not just the part), as well as a link with metaphor (Mike's life is likened to a continuous boat-trip). There is also a distinct overlap between hyperbole and some of the types of idioms we have considered above. To say that someone is *as slippery as an eel* is more exaggeratedly colourful than say *as slippery as a polished floor/an icy patch*. Other exaggerated idioms include *as quiet as a mouse, eagle-eyed, as sharp as a razor,* and *as strong as an ox* (for more examples, see Layton 1979).

INFORMATION ADD-ON

Much discussion has taken place in the literature concerning the overlap between hyperbole and metaphor. However, Rubio-Fernández et al. (2015) note that metaphor involves a transfer of meaning from the source domain to the target domain, while hyperbole involves no such transfer: *I have millions of cousins* stays in the domain of numbers if a person with twenty cousins is exaggerating.

It is far from straightforward to separate the various tropes in terms of their exploitations of figurative meaning in the lexicon. We have already seen how metaphor, metonymy, and idioms can be usefully studied together and as interacting; Colston and O'Brien (2000a) refer to these as 'families of tropes' which can have different pragmatic effects in contexts of use. So, in some ways, it is an artificial division to treat each trope separately and it is really no more than a convenient segmentation which reflects traditional approaches to these different figures of speech.

A NOT UNINTERESTING TROPE: UNDERSTATEMENT

Hyperbole involves overstatement, but the vocabulary can also be exploited in the opposite direction – understatement, where reality is down-toned rather than exaggerated, as Axel Hübler puts it, 'to say less than is meant' (Hübler 1983: 4). One way of doing this is through **litotes**. In rhetoric, litotes is a figure of speech which uses a negative to express the opposite meaning, often in an ironic way. The psycholinguist Herbert Colston contrasts an example of overstatement in 'This is the worst thing that could ever happen to anyone' with understatement in 'This is a bit unfortunate' (Colston 1997: 43). Understatement often involves a double negation. Here are some examples:

*The show was **not** an **un**qualified success.*
*They told her in **no un**certain terms that they were not happy.*
*I won't be **sorry** when it's all over.*

Other examples involve negatives together with superlatives:

*It wasn't the **best** meal I'd ever had and the service wasn't the **quickest** either.*
*She isn't the **easiest** person to get along with.*

Examples like these illustrate how, when making understatements, 'the speaker is somehow making the expected or desired state of affairs more salient when things have not turned out as expected and as a result, creates a contrast' (Colston and O'Brien 2000b: 1560).

CORPUS EVIDENCE

In a search of the BNC 1994 for *not* + negative adjectives beginning with *un-*, the following ten are the most frequent forms which are typically used in litotes.

1. not uncommon
2. not unusual
3. not unknown
4. not unreasonable
5. not unexpected
6. not unlikely
7. not untypical
8. not unhappy
9. not unpleasant
10. not unaware

In the past, understatement has often been seen as a typical British English trait – see the interesting discussion in Hübler (1983: 1–3). Whether that be true or not could only be resolved by comparing the rates and types of understatement in different languages, as well as establishing shared, rigorous criteria for investigating the trope across different languages and datasets. National stereotypes are usually unsubstantiated over-generalizations, and one might reasonably expect understatement as a communicative act to be a natural and perhaps universal social strategy rather than language- or culture-specific.

EUPHEMISMS

One last trope which involves exploiting the figurative potential of words and expressions is euphemism. **Euphemisms** involve using weaker or milder vocabulary instead of words and expressions which might be too harsh or direct in the context. Sensitive areas of our experience or potentially upsetting or offence-causing language are avoided. For example, from events connected with death we may say that someone has *passed away* or *has left us* or *is no longer with us*. Soldiers who have died in a war or conflict might be referred to as *the fallen*, while accidentally injuring or killing troops from your own side or allies is called a *blue-on-blue* incident (Chovanec 2019). Animals and birds are *culled* instead of *killed* to control their populations or they are *(big) game* for hunters, while they are *prey* when other animals or birds kill them (for more examples of euphemisms concerning animals, see Trampe 2018).

Euphemisms may be sometimes used for humorous effect (*to powder one's nose* or *to spend a penny* instead of 'go to the toilet') or simply for polite avoidance of directly naming something (*the restroom, the bathroom, the washroom, the loo*). They can also be used to 'soften a blow', as in a 2022 announcement by Google informing users of the closure of one of its services, which ran, 'We will begin to *sunset* Universal Analytics in 2023' (Google email to customers 19 April 2022 – my italics). However, euphemisms can lose their force over time and become 'contaminated' by the very meaning they are trying to soften, so that, as McGlone et al. put it, 'This process eventually drives them out of conversational circulation and leads to the creation of new euphemisms to replace them' (McGlone et al. 2006: 262). What were some years back generally referred to as *disabled* toilet facilities for people with physical mobility problems are now usually referred to as *accessible* facilities. This is a good example of how vocabulary changes to suit changing social perceptions – we are less likely to stress the potentially upsetting, negative physical abilities of people and instead show sensitivity by highlighting their needs and rights to access public facilities and amenities.

SUMMARY

In this chapter, we have moved from an initial consideration of what it means to refer to the 'literal' meaning of words, through a discussion of how meaning can spread across several words – the chunks which have fixed forms and unitary meanings. We then went on to look at how chunks often have idiomatic (non-transparent) meanings and how we perceive and decode those meanings. This led us to a discussion of metaphor and metonymy, and how these tropes pervade our ordinary, everyday use of vocabulary. Other tropes we looked at, such as hyperbole, understatement, and euphemism, lead us to the inevitable conclusion that figurative language is not something obscure that belongs to poetry or high literature, but that much of our everyday communication is based on figurative meanings. Figurative meanings help us to conceptually organize and make sense of our environment and experiences. But how does what goes on in our minds relate to the words and chunks which we must have in there somewhere, stored in our brains ready for use? This will be the subject of Chapter 5.

FURTHER READING

Deignan, A. 2005. *Metaphor and Corpus Linguistics*. Amsterdam: John Benjamins.
Since metaphor has underlain a lot of the discussion in this chapter, Alice Deignan's book would be a good follow-up text to read next. Deignan tackles a complex subject in a clear style in the first part of the book, where she covers both metaphor and metonymy. Part II then takes us into the world of real corpus data with a wealth of examples.

Moon, R. 1998. *Fixed Expressions and Idioms in English*. Oxford: Clarendon Press.
Rosamund Moon's book is a comprehensive, corpus-based study of all types of idiomatic expressions, including those discussed in this chapter and many more. It is full of clear, useful examples from real texts and covers both the forms, meanings, and discourse functions of idioms, as well as the tropes (e.g., metaphor, hyperbole) which we have touched upon in this chapter. It is an essential read for anyone interested in idioms and other aspects of figurative meaning.

Sinclair, J. 1991. *Corpus, Concordance, Collocation.* **Oxford: Oxford University Press.**

John Sinclair's book was a pioneering text with regard to how meaning spreads over more than one word, and how we can observe language chunks in corpora operating as single choices (the idiom principle) instead of always seeing the creation of meaning as a word-by-word process. It remains one of the most important books in the area.

NOTE

1 https://www.macmillandictionary.com/dictionary/british/join-the-dots.

BEAR THIS IN MIND
THE MENTAL LEXICON

A REMARKABLE ACHIEVEMENT

At birth, a child knows no words. By age two, they are typically able to produce anything up to a thousand words (Nation and Coxhead 2021: 7). By age seven, the age when many children around the world start school properly, we can expect an English-native-speaking child to know about 5,000 word families. A **word family** is usually defined as a basic word-form and all its related derivations, so, for example, *beauty, beautiful, beautifully, beautify,* and *beautification* all belong to the same word family. This is different from lemmas. In Chapter 1, we saw that a lemma was the base form of a word and its inflected forms (e.g., plural/past tense/-*ing* form) all brought together, for example, *speak, speaks, spoke, speaking,* and *spoken*. A word family is a broader definition which takes derived forms – forms with prefixes and suffixes – into account.

With reasonable life chances and schooling, the child/young person's vocabulary will go on growing at about 1,000 word families a year and this will continue, to the extent that an educated adult may be able to handle anything from 30,000 to 50,000 word families. What is more, there is no reason to believe that vocabulary acquisition has a cut-off age, and it can continue till the end of a person's life. The figures are to be taken as general guidelines since they depend on the different possible ways of defining what counts as a 'word' or 'word family', what the child's environment is, and the richness of interaction with adults the child is exposed to. Not least, also, is the question of what we mean when we say someone *knows* a word. Whatever method we use to arrive at a final tally, it

DOI: 10.4324/9781003284611-6

is generally agreed in the literature that the figures quoted above are a reliable weathervane of typical vocabulary development. From zero vocabulary to tens of thousands of items is a remarkable feat.

CORPUS EVIDENCE

If we consider a corpus such as the British National Corpus (BNC 1994) to be a reliable snapshot of the words which were in circulation when the data were collected, we find 33,711 lemmas which occur 50 or more times in the 90 million words of texts collected between 1985 and 1993. There is a huge 'tail' of hundreds of thousands of lemmas which occur between 1 and 49 times – those occurring only a handful of times will be rare or specialized technical and scientific words which not many people will ever encounter, understand, or use.

The evidence points to at least 33,000 'dictionary headwords' being in everyday circulation in newspapers, books, magazines, and recorded speech in the last part of the twentieth century. They are words which most adult native speakers of British English who have gone through normal education will understand and use when needed. And some speakers will have a command of many more words.

HOW DID IT ALL GET THERE? ACQUIRING VOCABULARY

DESIGNING A HUMAN

If a typical English speaker has acquired a vocabulary of tens of thousands of words by the time they become adults, how did this come about? One possible answer is that the new-born child comes into the world predisposed to acquire language, that we are genetically equipped in a way that other animals are not. The American linguist Noam Chomsky, in one of his earliest works on grammar, challenged the idea that acquiring a language was just 'behaviour', no more than a response to environmental stimuli, in the way a circus animal might perform for rewards. Chomsky said: 'The fact that all normal children acquire essentially comparable grammars of great complexity with remarkable rapidity suggests that human beings are somehow specially designed to do this'

(Chomsky 1959: 57); he could equally well have been talking about the acquisition of vocabulary.

Whatever is the precise nature of the human genetic predisposition to learn vocabulary, children still need exposure to an environment which will determine whether they acquire English, Thai, Finnish, Swahili, or any other language. They may even be in an environment where they are exposed to and acquire the vocabularies of two, three, or more languages, i.e., **bilingual**, **trilingual**, or **multilingual** lexicons. The environment and input from caregivers, other children, and other adults is essential for the acquisition of vocabulary. Nowadays, audio-visual input from films, TV, games, and other electronic stimuli also plays a part in exposing children to vocabulary.

Above all, conversation and interaction are the key factors in 'learning how to mean' in a language. *Learning how to Mean* is the title of an important work by the British linguist Michael Halliday. Halliday followed the progress of his own son from his earliest days as the child made sense of his social environment and developed an understanding of the functions of the words and grammar he was exposed to through interaction. Halliday's focus is more on what the child learns to *do* with language, i.e., a social view of acquisition, rather than the mental/cognitive representations of the language (Halliday 1975).

ONE WORD AT A TIME

Children listen before they can speak and absorb language like a sponge. When they start to use their vocal cords in language-like ways, it is usually through what is known as **cooing** and (at a later stage) **babbling**, that is to say they begin to combine vowel and consonant sounds (e.g., *goo-goo*) and can produce sequences such as *ba-ba* and *ma-ma* before they are a year old. For an example of a child exercising her vocal cords in this way, see Carter and McCarthy (1997: 129). *Ba-ba* and *ma-ma* are not chosen randomly here as examples: b- and m- sounds emerge as the most frequent first vocal articulations in a wide range of languages around the world (Locke 1986).

When a child moves from the cooing and babbling stage, words begin to form, single ones at first, but a single word can perform different functions in context: *Teddy!* could mean 'I want my teddy bear', or 'this is my teddy bear', or 'there's a teddy bear in the shop-window', and so on. First words may include versions of adult words, learnt from what is referred to as **baby talk** or **child-directed speech (CDS)** or **caretaker speech**, with reduplication, rhyme, and musicality playing a part, for example, onomatopoeic animal names such as *bow-wow, gee-gee, moo-cow/moo-moo, quack-quack, baa-lamb*, as well as names with *-y*-endings (*piggy, doggy, horsey, birdy, bunny*). Names such as these and the names of other things in the child's immediate environment (often referred to as the ***here-and-now***) become crucial in the child's vocabulary development. A very famous article, published in 1958 by Roger Brown, encapsulates this in its title: *How shall a thing be called?* Brown begins his discussion saying:

> The most deliberate part of first-language teaching is the business of telling a child what each thing is called. We ordinarily speak of the name of a thing as if there were just one, but in fact, of course, every referent has many names.
>
> (Brown 1958: 14)

He then goes on to explain the significance of the different names for the same referent in the child's language development:

> The dog out on the lawn is not only a dog but is also a *boxer*, a *quadruped*, an *animate being*; it is the landlord's dog, named *Prince*. How will it be identified for a child? Sometimes it will be called a *dog*, sometimes *Prince*, less often a *boxer*, and almost never a *quadruped*, or *animate being*.
>
> (Brown, ibid.)

This suggests that there is a pragmatic dimension to the naming of people and things in the child's learning environment, which relates back to our discussion in Chapter 3 concerning levels of lexical specificity and the salience of core terms. Brown also points out that shorter or monosyllabic words such as *dog* are not only easier for the child to imitate and assimilate but are also likely to be the most frequent terms. In English, there is definitely a pay-off between word-length and frequency, with long words of many syllables being usually of lower frequency. Thus, the child's learning environment is scaffolded by the adult's judicious choice of simple names.

What is more, the child often hears multiple occurrences of a word or phrase, from adults and from siblings and other, older children. Catherine Snow refers to the way the parent (mothers in the cases she refers to) 'frequently repeated phrases and whole sentences and paraphrased their own utterances' (Snow 1986: 70). Snow also argues that the simplified register of CDS stimulates the attention of the child and that complex, unfamiliar sentences can be 'filtered out'. This, she points out, challenges strong claims that a hard-wired predisposed genetic language acquisition device is the key driver in language acquisition and argues for recognition of the role of interaction and CDS. CDS may help the innate faculty to operate more efficiently. Snow goes on to say, in reference to the importance of the *here-and-now*:

> Mothers make statements and ask questions about what things are called, what noises they make, what colour they are, what actions they are engaging in, who they belong to, where they are located, and very little else.
>
> (Snow 1986: 78)

Through interaction and exposure to repeated occurrences of words, the child learns names for whole classes of people and things and starts to apply them to its environment. Sometimes **over-extension** of meaning occurs: the child may think that all dogs can be referred to as *Prince* or *Rover* or whatever their own family pet is called. Sometimes, the opposite will apply: the child may hesitate to call an example of an unfamiliar-looking breed a *dog*, a case of **under-extension**. Over-extension often happens with grammatical forms, especially regular verb endings, so that a child may say *it's falled* (fallen) or *we goed* (went). Over time, through repeated experience, the child learns the semantic limits of a word and the conventions of its grammar (Figure 5.1).

The young child also has to grapple increasingly with more difficult sounds and their pronunciation. A member of my own family when very small would refer to the colour yellow as *lellow* and to binoculars as *pinocklias* but over a relatively short space of time learnt

Figure 5.1 Baby talk. © Jake Tebbit 2022.

the conventional pronunciation. Consonant clusters may prove particularly difficult in words such as *train*, *friend*, *that's*, which may be articulated as *twain*, *fwiend* and *das*.

CORPUS EVIDENCE

The 0–3 years-old, 4.5-million-word segment of the Childes English Corpus (a collection of conversations involving children of different ages) has 51 examples of *lellow*, which the adult interlocutor often corrects to *yellow*. Here is an example of a child two years and three months old identifying colours:

<adult> okay. what colour is that?
<child> dat's lellow.
<adult> yellow?
<child> lellow.
<adult> that's good. alright.

(doc. 5913. From sub-corpus known as the Warren Corpus. For information on the corpus, see Warren-Leubecker and Bohannon 1984.)

TELEGRAMS FROM A CHILD

Another step in the development of the child's vocabulary comes in picking up two-word chunks such as *all gone, this one, that one, fall down*, which although they may look as if they are grammatically 'assembled' (*all* + past participle; demonstrative + substitute pronoun; phrasal verb) are processed and used as chunks. The linguists Laura De Ruiter and Anna Theakston put it this way:

> Once children begin to talk, there is ample evidence that their early word combinations appear to be lexically specific, item-based constructions, known as 'frozen phrases' or 'schemas.' Frozen phrases are unanalyzed combinations of words that always appear together in that form, with no evidence of flexibility in use, such as *I dunno* or *What's that?*
>
> (De Ruiter and Theakston 2017: 61)

These fixed chunks may be exploited functionally in different contexts. For example, the child might say *Teddy all gone* if the teddy bear is hidden, *Tommy all gone* if the family pet exits the room, by analogy with *All gone!* when food is finished and the plate is empty. This stage of putting two or three words together is often referred to as **telegraphic speech**, like the economic use of words in an old-fashioned telegram where you paid per word. But by the age of three to five years, full clauses are common which show evidence of assembly in real time, for example, *I don't know where x is/I don't want you to* + verb, and the earliest chunks may only be analysed syntactically at a later stage (if ever), through formal grammar lessons at school. Alison Wray, writing about formulaic chunks of various kinds in child language, says of two important types:

> Other strings are formulaic for many people in the speech community, normally because they have learned them from each other: such sequences are better *not* analyzed, because they may be irregular, and also because they are the mainstay of idiomaticity, so the child needs to store them whole. Finally, some formulaic material is more decisively formulaic. It is institutionalized and derives its power from the fixedness of its form, so, again, the child will gain little and could lose a lot by analyzing it.
>
> (Wray 2002: 129)

Even in the earliest child language, we see evidence of Sinclair's idiom principle in operation which we discussed in Chapter 4.

MORE THAN ONE WAY OF SAYING THINGS

Some children are exposed to more than one language. In the bilingual environment, if the child has more or less equal exposure to both languages, they are likely to acquire a balanced control of both, with two lexicons available for use, each in its own usual contexts. They become **balanced bilinguals**. But the bilingual lexicon is not always a 50-50 affair, and the lexicons may be unbalanced. Another factor which scholars take into consideration is whether the two languages are learnt at the same time (**simultaneous bilingualism**) or one after the other (**sequential bilingualism**). Bilingual children who have progressed to producing clauses and sentences may occasionally mix in words from the other language while speaking primarily in one of the two (see examples in Silva-Corvalán 2014: ch.3). In discussing trilingual speakers, one group of researchers concludes:

> Separate languages do not appear to have their own distinct substrates in the brain, and psycholinguistic research also shows that languages cannot be completely switched off, which can be interpreted as evidence for an integrated system. However, at the same time, the fact that multilinguals can choose to use one and not the other language shows that the systems can be separated.
>
> (Rothman et al. 2013: 383)

Whether balanced or unbalanced, simultaneous or sequential, the acquisition of two or more lexicons makes the general achievement of vocabulary growth in the early years impressive, to say the least. Nor is bilingualism rare: millions of people around the world operate in more than one language on a daily basis, and the spread of English as a *lingua franca* and increasing mobility and contact between languages through globalization means that bilingual, trilingual, and multilingual (or **plurilingual**) societies are to be found everywhere (see Stavans and Hoffmann 2015).

SPELL IT OUT

Given what the child has to cope with in the early years (new words, new meanings, new sounds, new grammar, learning to walk, coordinating sensory-motor skills), it is remarkable that by age five, a child may be able to use with aplomb around 3,000 words. Then comes schooling, with encounters with increasing numbers of written texts where the challenge of English spelling and orthography are faced. The alphabet has to be matched to a bewildering range of consonant and vowel sounds, and the sound-spelling mismatches that lead to the unpredictability of so many English words have to be tackled. As we saw in Chapter 2, English spelling became historically 'stuck' thanks to standardization. The spelling of many words remained unchanged but over the centuries, the pronunciation shifted. Sound, spelling, meaning, all are taken on board, processed, and stored in memory for near-instantaneous retrieval as and when needed.

INFORMATION ADD-ON

Here are some examples of sound-spelling mismatches in English which may cause problems in writing or pronunciation for children (and for many adults too!).

fork and *work*   *hood* and *food*   *new* and *sew*   *month* and *moth*
flower and *lower* *glove* and *stove* *bough* and *though* *comb* and *tomb*

Somehow, miraculously, vocabulary acquisition happens, mostly unconsciously in the pre-school years, and the whole enterprise recedes into near total oblivion as we grow up, with only the briefest occasional flashback to the language experiences of our earliest years. Somehow, in those first years, our vocabulary expands massively but expands in what way? Where? In our brains, yes, but in what form? Cells and molecules? Electrical charges? Where? How? Unfortunately, none of these questions has an easy or straightforward answer.

WHERE ARE ALL THOSE WORDS?

MIND AND BRAIN: THE MENTAL LEXICON

We know that the many thousands of word families we have at our disposal are stored and processed in the human brain (rather than in our spine or heart) and are a feature of what we call our **mind** – the faculty of being able to experience things, to think about them, to articulate them, and act upon them, in this case through language, and, specifically, through using our vocabulary. The mind is the psychological manifestation of the activity of the physical brain. But it is quite overwhelming to consider how tens of thousands of items can be all stored away in our heads. And note that, so far, we have only considered tentative statistics for word families that children acquire over the formative years (most likely 15,000–16,000 word-families by the age of 18). Acquisition of new words goes on into adult life. Then add to those figures the many chunks, idioms, etc. which we discussed in Chapter 4, and the picture becomes even more staggering, with perhaps 50,000–60,000 lexical items available to an educated adult (Aitchison 2012: 8). To make sense of these impressive facts, we instinctively turn to the kinds of conceptual metaphors we discussed in Chapter 4. Metaphors for the human mind typically see it as a centre (physical and/or virtual) where vocabulary is stored and processed. We will from now on refer to that centre of operations as the **mental lexicon**.

To approach how the mind stores and processes vocabulary, we might conceptualize it different ways, for example, THE MIND IS A REPOSITORY, THE MIND IS A COMPUTER, THE MIND IS A NETWORK, or THE MIND IS A PLACE/A LANDSCAPE (Figure 5.2).

All of these metaphors can serve as ways of grasping the extraordinary facility humans possess automatically to comprehend and retrieve vocabulary almost instantaneously from an apparently massive store of items. Note how easily I slip into the idea of a 'store', and how convenient it is to think of the mind as a sort of container.

- CONTAINER: The mind, from this perspective, could be seen as a dictionary where words are 'stored' and we 'look up' information about the words we produce or receive, or like a

Figure 5.2 Metaphors of the mind. © Jake Tebbit 2022.

library catalogue where we search the details of a book before finding it stored on its shelf (Aitchison 2012: 37).

- COMPUTER: Information about words is stored on a hard drive (the brain), while the 'address' of each word is a non-physical set of binary codes which together make up the word's instantly retrievable profile using the minimum number of keystrokes or the click of a mouse.
- NETWORK: One word and its form and meaning are linked in a series of neural connections or electrical charges to other words and to concepts, all operating in the largely invisible systems of the brain, as invisible as a complex underground electric railway when we are up there on the street (see Aitchison 2012: ch.9).
- PLACE: The mind is like a place, a populated landscape, where the locations of stored words can be close to each other or distant from each other, and where they can move and shift about on its map, occupying different environments over time and through repeated experiences. This would be just like people moving around a city but where everyone carries a smartphone and is instantly and mutually contactable.

As our scientific knowledge evolves, we may increasingly come to compare the mind to a quantum-physical world where particles behave in mysterious ways and can't be pinned down to any state or identity until they are measured! Words might behave like particles, and a well-designed vocabulary test or experiment would be our version of 'measurement' and would be equally tentative and provisional. For a discussion on this and other science-based metaphors of the mind, see Turvey and Moreno (2006).

REFLECTION POINT

Consider these everyday uses of the word *mind*. What types of metaphors do they encapsulate?

What's on your mind?
I'll bear that in mind
I can see it in my mind's eye
What springs to mind when you hear the word 'autumn'?
My mind is all over the place at the moment.
He changed his mind at the last minute.

HOW DOES IT WORK?

In one of the most important works on the mental lexicon, Jean Aitchison discusses the problems associated with modelling invisible processes (one example she gives is understanding what is going on in the core of the sun), how scientific modelling often requires some guesswork, and how modelling the mental lexicon is not immune to the same problems. We can create a tentative model, conduct experiments, and test our hypotheses using different methods but cannot be sure from the results that we have fully exposed the underlying processes. As outside observers of the human brain and mind, we cannot be completely certain as to what is happening on the inside (Aitchison 2012: 34–36). Aitchison discusses the metaphor of the library (see above) and how books and methods of locating them could be arranged in different ways. She asks:

> Are all words to be regarded as equal? Or are frequent words and rare words treated differently? Each analogy, therefore, can provide researchers with a whole range of ideas for testing.
>
> (Aitchison 2012: 37)

The mention of tests reminds us of the metaphor of quantum physics, where nothing is real until we measure it, and the elusive reality of the quantum world may turn out to be a sound if bewildering metaphor for the mental lexicon (Bruza et al. 2009).

The linguists Karen Emmorey and Victoria Fromkin describe the makeup of the mental lexicon as:

> ... all the information - phonological, morphological, semantic, and syntactic – that speakers know about individual words and/or morphemes'
>
> (Emmorey and Fromkin 1988: 124).

Another researcher cites a similar definition (before he seriously challenges it) that the mental lexicon is 'a kind of dictionary that contains information regarding a word's meaning, pronunciation, syntactic characteristics, and so on' (Elman 2004: 301). Both of these definitions point up the complexity of what it means to 'know' a word, and in both cases we can add a great deal more information that we carry in our heads about words, including typical and untypical collocations, idiom-proneness, appropriateness for use in different registers (e.g., level of formality, whether the item is current or archaic), whether it belongs to a particular dialect or variety, its cultural connotations, its productivity in terms of attracting prefixes and suffixes, its use in compounds, whether it has homonyms and homographs, its degree of coreness or salience, its prototypicality, a general sense of its frequency or rarity – all the many aspects of vocabulary items which we have discussed in Chapters 1–4 of this book. In short, if the mental lexicon is like a dictionary, it is way more complex and sophisticated than any printed or online dictionary to date.

One thing we can observe, however, is that, for most people, the lexicon can be accessed both for comprehension and production almost instantaneously, albeit we may occasionally be hesitant or 'at a loss for words'. Because of this, a store of 50,000–60,000 items is highly unlikely to be just a random list of unconnected, individual 'addresses'. That would seem incredibly inefficient. But, if it is systematically organized in some way, what is likely to be the nature of such organization, and what kinds of plausible evidence can we gather to help us understand it?

FASTER THAN YOU CAN SAY JACK ROBINSON

Tests and experiments of various kinds have been used to gauge how informants access their mental lexicons. These include word recognition tests and various types of word association tests (see Aitchison 2012: 8–11, 27–28, 100–101). Through these techniques, it is generally believed that the external behaviour of informants in some way reflects their internal lexicon and how it is accessed and organized. In **word recognition** tests, for example, the informants are asked whether a string of sounds they listen to is a word in that language or not, and mostly they are able to decide yes or no remarkably quickly, in under half a second, speedily and confidently rejecting sound sequences that are non-words, even though there may occasionally be borderline cases which cause hesitation. Access to words and non-words is, in most cases, virtually instantaneous.

The mental lexicon is not like a big box full of hundreds of books thrown in in no particular order, where you have to rummage through the entire pile to find a book you need, which may be right at the bottom of the box. Any book, once you've consulted it and successfully stored away the key information, can be accessed as fast as any other book. That is not to say that there are not obscure or unfamiliar words which may take a while to remember or which we may only half understand. In my case, *jejune, deleterious, palimpsest, pellucid, adumbrate,* and *chiliastic* all cause me to hesitate or else I have to look them up now and again to recall their meanings. But compared to the tens of thousands of words I can use or understand instantly, these are rare exceptions.

A great amount of research has been conducted into word recognition, going right back to the end of the nineteenth century. Studies have ranged from how children from the earliest ages onwards recognize words, how people with disabilities fare in recognition tasks, how the development of reading skills is affected by word recognition, how ageing affects people's recognition abilities, how text and context, familiarity, and repeated exposure to words affect speed of recognition, how tests can reveal differences between first and second-language acquisition, and so on.

REFLECTION POINT

How quickly can you recognize English words and non-words from this list? Are there any which are borderline cases?

*anvil   clollpra   stentorian   conspicuousness   frinble   chewnosk
    loppish   nonchalant*

In reading, it is not enough just to recognize a string of characters or to say yes or no as to whether it is a word or a non-word. Reading is a complex process whereby substance, the written form (orthography) is transformed into sound (a phonological representation) – whether we are reading aloud or silently – and then we have to relate this to a meaning (a semantic representation). This is the classic form-to-meaning process. Producing language, writing and speaking, goes the other way: meaning has to be articulated as form (words) and substance, either writing or speech. And the process is not just a straight-line in either direction. Omer Ari, a researcher interested in college-age adults' word-recognition skills in reading, describes the form-meaning trajectory as a more complex affair:

> This involves a three-way connection: (a) between the spelling and sound of the word; (b) between the spelling and meaning of the word; and (c) between the sound and meaning of the word. Once established for a given word, an amalgam of this sort results in effortless recognition of the word in and out of context.

(Ari 2016: 719)

The experience of the child acquiring language will be dominated by learning sound-to-meaning relationships. Only later will the child encounter books and writing and take on the challenge of the three-way relationship as described by Ari.

The process is indeed complex, and it is likely that the form-to-meaning process is not a straight-line; rather, the various sub-processes of seeing/hearing a word, recognizing it as a word, and knowing which word it is (lexical access), then accessing its meaning, may overlap in time for maximum efficiency. The weakest link may be that between the lexical representation and the meaning, especially if semantic memory is slow or poorly organized (Chabot et al. 1984). Figure 5.3 shows how the overlapping processes might work for form to meaning; remarkably, for most words, they all normally happen in milliseconds.

WHAT COMES INTO YOUR HEAD?

Along with word-recognition experiments, another procedure which has a long history aimed at understanding how the mental lexicon is organized is **word association** tests. You may have done one of these yourself. They work by the experimenter feeding the informant a list of stimulus words to which they have to react immediately and say the first word that comes into their mind. The fact that many people give the same responses to stimulus words has been taken to mean that we share ways of organizing vocabulary in our minds. If 100 people all say *down* when they hear the word *up*, this might suggest that words are stored not only partly as antonymous sets, but also partly as sets of prepositions/adverbs of direction and motion. If *black* typically gets the response *white*, this may suggest an organization based on antonyms and on a general store of adjectives, but it could also suggest a tighter stored lexical set of

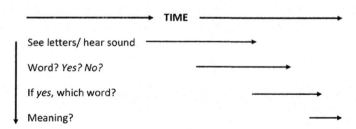

Figure 5.3 Form to meaning.

colour terms, or even social and cultural associations. *Red* and *green* may not only be strongly associated as adjectives of colour but may also be associated through shared experience of traffic-light systems. *Bell* may provoke *ring*, but *ring*, in its turn may spark *wedding*. People can *ring* bells and bells can *ring*; these are **syntagmatic** associations, relations of syntax, e.g., between a subject and object (*ring a bell*) or a pre-modifier and a noun (*wedding ring*). *Red, yellow, blue, green, black,* and *white* and *up, down, across, over,* and *under* are in **paradigmatic** relationships with one another; they belong to lexical sets. *Weddings* and *rings* belong more generally to the same semantic field of 'getting married'.

As we can see from these example responses, the behaviour of informants in word association tests might be predictable, but the explanation may be more elusive. As Susan Ervin pointed out more than six decades ago, the words fed to informants in word association tasks are typically words they have seen before and which have contextual associations of varying degrees, whether through repeated syntactic patterns (*cup of tea, cup of coffee; front door, back door*) or just general experience of a range of contexts (Ervin 1961). Words can even be associated simply by existing in the same 'semantic neighbourhood', even though their semantic components may be only loosely related: Buchanan and Westbury (2001: 532) cite *scratch* and *cat* as examples of this looser association. Note how 'neighbourhood' chimes with the metaphor of the mental lexicon being like a place.

REFLECTION POINT

Try this word association test on yourself and on any willing volunteer(s). What could the results possibly tell us about the ways in which word are organized in the mind? Are some words more likely to prompt a more immediate response than others?

thick   walk   lamp   towards   cup   lie   armchair   sunny   sing branch
immediate   vase   here   shopping   passport   door   oversee thunder   rose

Ervin also discusses **clang responses**, that is when a response to a stimulus word is based on sound, producing rhymes such as *boy -> toy, fly -> pie, sea -> tree*, etc. (Ervin 1961). These are age-related, with children producing more clang associations than adults. As the child's mental lexicon becomes more organized, association by meaning takes over increasingly from association by sound.

Not all words are equally strongly associated with one another: *planet* is more likely statistically to produce the response *earth* than the response *mars*, even though both may occur, and some words have more associated words than others, stronger links, and greater connectivity in word networks (Bruza et al. 2009). However, in broad terms, word association does seem to tell us something about how the mental lexicon is organized; what is more, some of the types of responses mentioned here that have emerged from English word association tests also seem to emerge from similar tests in other languages (Rosenzweig 1961).

Tess Fitzpatrick and Peter Thwaites, two researchers who specialize in the acquisition of vocabulary by learners of English as a second or foreign language, say, 'Word association research is deceptively simple' (Fitzpatrick and Thwaites 2020: 237). *Deceptively simple* suggests that the field is anything but simple. Some of the complications we have considered include:

- How familiar the cue words are for the respondents
- Whether responses are paradigmatic or syntagmatic
- Whether a response is based on sense relations or word class
- Whether responses belong more loosely to a shared semantic field
- How social and cultural connotations of words may affect responses
- Whether some words have stronger links between them than other words in the same lexical set
- How age might affect the response (e.g., clang responses)

In another article, Fitzpatrick and her co-researchers question the generalizability of word association results, especially relating to age, but also relating to the comparability of norms used in such research (for example, using native-speaker norms in research into second-language use). They say:

> ... the focus has not been on capturing a range of normal behaviours so much as on interpreting the behaviour of an individual in relation to assumed normal responses.
>
> (Fitzpatrick et al. 2015: 24)

Word association information tells us a lot about how the mental lexicon may be organized, but it doesn't tell the whole story and by no means captures the psychological complexity of vocabulary storage and use.

JUST A SLIP OF THE TONGUE?

Why do people sometimes get a word *almost* right? Sometimes, especially in high-stress situations, speakers stumble over words or say a word which is very similar to what they want to say but is not the right word to express their meaning. Here are two examples from the time of writing where radio interviewees were responding to urgent questions about a simmering international conflict:

Intelligence suggests that an invasion is eminent.
Among the general population there is no atmosphere for war.

In the first example, the speaker clearly meant to say *imminent*; the stress of the moment may have led to a wrong choice of words, but what is noticeable is that *eminent* and *imminent* differ in only one vowel sound. The speaker sounded highly educated and gave no reason to believe they did not know the difference between *eminent* and *imminent*. In the second example, *atmosphere* fits the meaning adequately enough, and yet, for me at least, the normal collocation would be *no appetite for war*. Indeed, an internet search for *no atmosphere for war* yielded just one result, while *no appetite for war* yielded more than 200,000 hits.

These examples of not hitting the right word may be put down to **slips of the tongue**: we cannot necessarily conclude that the speakers' vocabulary is confused or impoverished in some way. Two researchers in phonetics showed that slips of the tongue involving the replacement of a sound (such as we saw in *imminent* > *eminent*) were perceived by informants far less frequently than those involving other types of difference, including unintentional blends (e.g., saying *trollies* as a blend of *trucks* and *lorries*) transposing sounds (*chish and fips* instead of *fish and chips*) and replacement of one word by another, as we saw with *appetite* > *atmosphere* (Tent and Clark 1980). In a 2022 BBC Radio 4 debate on the subject of landscape rewilding in England, an interviewee, when challenged that such a move would be a retrograde step, replied, 'It's not about turning the clack, the clock back', clear evidence of immediate retrieval of an entire idiomatic expression, transposing the vowel sound of *back* to *clock*.

However, detecting slips of the tongue, especially in real-time listening as opposed to repeated playing of recordings, is not a straightforward task (see Ferber 1995 for a discussion). Most slips of the tongue do not interfere with the overall meaning of the message. They are interesting from the point of view of speech production in real time and they underline yet again the complexity of accessing and retrieving items, both single words and expressions, from the mental lexicon.

Another kind of 'slip' is referred to as **slips of the ear** (Cutler 1981: 566). This happens when we think we have heard a particular word or phrase but then, with more context, we realize we have heard wrongly. Two recent examples that I have experienced listening to the radio are the following:

Initial hearing	corrected after more context
A tax on asylum seekers…	Attacks on asylum seekers have increased recently.
The discovery of split jeans …	The discovery of split genes led to the award of the Nobel Prize in Physiology or Medicine in 1993.

In both cases, it was a matter of no more than a second before I realized I had misheard, further evidence of how quickly word processing takes place in the mental lexicon and the importance of context (Figure 5.4).

Some replacements of words lead to obviously wrong and usually humorous outcomes. The speaker may genuinely believe that they are using the correct word. These are **malapropisms**, and we shall look at some examples in Chapter 6.

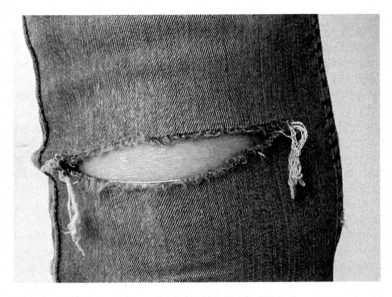

Figure 5.4 Split genes. Image © Michael McCarthy 2022.

IN TWO MINDS AGAIN

We mentioned earlier the fact that many people in the world are bilingual, trilingual, or multilingual. Furthermore, at any given moment, millions of people around the world are attempting to learn English as a second or foreign language (**L2 learners**). Much of the research we have looked at in relation to first-language acquisition has been replicated in the context of bilingual, trilingual, and multilingual speakers, as well as with L2 learners. Such methods include experiments in word recognition, word association, and, in the case of L2 learners, lexical errors and lexical transfer. These methods are often used in connexion with estimates of L2 learners' vocabulary size and how best L2 learners can grow their vocabulary.

In the case of bilinguals, a question that has been investigated is how two words that are translation equivalents are stored in the mental lexicon. One attempt to answer the question is the **separate storage** model: 'The separate storage model postulates two separate language-specific representational systems. Each of the words in a translation pair has its own conceptual representation' (Dong et al. 2005: 221). Dong et al. argue that this has not proved to be a satisfactory account of the bilingual mental lexicon, with inconsistencies in the evidence for how different types of words are stored. Concrete words seem to be linked more closely in the two languages than abstract words. Dong et al. then discuss the **concept-mediation model**, which stresses a 'single language-neutral representation for each concept and that L2 words access this representation directly' (Dong et al. 2005: 222). They conclude that the evidence points to one single conceptual store in the bilingual's mental lexicon, but that the most satisfactory model is a dynamic one which responds to change over time: other scholars also agree on a more integrated mental lexicon for those engaging with more than one language; for example, Libben (2000: 230) refers to a 'homogenous lexical architecture'.

However, we cannot assume that models of the lexicon which were based on (a) access to single words and (b) the behaviour of monolingual speakers must be equally valid with regard to those who speak more than one language or who are L2 learners. Nor can we assume that such models are valid for the acquisition of chunks and how chunks relate to one another in the mental lexicon with more than one language. There is also the question of changing patterns of storage and access as bilingual speakers and L2 learners develop greater fluency, just as happens in first-language learning as children mature. Furthermore, among tri-lingual and multilingual speakers, one language is often stronger and more proficient than the others, and vocabulary processing may act differently in each language, while L2 learners may come to depend less on their first language as a route in and out of meaning and develop more direct links between L2 words and their meanings.

In 2003, my co-researcher Carol Spöttl and I published a paper where we looked at whether and how L2 learners noticed chunks (multi-word items) in English texts. We found that, by and large, success in the task was influenced by how salient or opaque the chunks were, and by general language proficiency (Spöttl and McCarthy 2003). A year later, we looked back on that study and concluded:

> Without a certain level of general language proficiency, noticing did not even take place and participants were found to completely ignore sections of L2 dialogues containing multiword items.
>
> (Spőttl and McCarthy 2004: 193)

However, in our 2004 paper, we were able to see how advanced-level multilingual speakers reacted in their different languages to encounters with chunks in English dialogues and how accessing meaning holistically (as opposed to taking the chunk apart word-by-word) could often then be translated holistically into a chunk in the participants' other languages. Experiments of this type suggest that the bilingual and multilingual mental lexicons can access the meaning of chunks and link them across different languages.

CONCLUSION

This chapter has covered the basics of an immensely complicated feature of human mental activity. It by no means conveys fully the complexity of our ability to absorb, process, memorize, and use tens of thousands of words and chunks, nor can it adequately address how these processes can happen in mere milliseconds. Most people not suffering from disabilities take for granted that thoughts can be expressed in words, immediately, in real time, in speech or writing, and that the sounds we hear and letters we read can equally quickly go the other way, to become words and chunks which have meanings. Understanding where all these words and chunks exist in our minds can usually only be grasped through metaphors.

The mental lexicon may be an expanding library or an online dictionary, it may be a computer, it may be a delicate network, it may be a place, a populated, bustling landscape, or an elusive quantum-physical zone. Whichever metaphor we feel attracted to, it would be unwise to think of the mental lexicon as fixed and stable. It may be a library, but old, dusty books will sometimes have to make way for new acquisitions. It may be a dictionary, but it is a fluid one, where words drop out and new ones come in. It may be a computer, but it is one where new data are added constantly and superfluous data dumped in the recycle bin. If it is a network, new connections among its nodes are being built all the time; some are strengthened, others weaken or stand idle. If it is a place, it is like a city where new roads, bridges, and buildings are added, and others altered and removed in the restless tide of human activity. If it is a quantum-physical phenomenon, we may have to be satisfied by apparently contradictory and puzzling realities. The dynamic nature of each of these metaphors comes about by the fact that vocabulary has no existence or *raison d'être* outside of society, which itself is not fixed or stable, and is constantly changed through social action. It is to vocabulary in action in the social world that we must finally turn our attention in Chapter 6.

FURTHER READING

Aitchison, J. 2012. *Words in the Mind: An Introduction to the Mental Lexicon*. Fourth edition. Oxford: Wiley-Blackwell.
Jean Aitchison's book, originally published in 1987, remains the best work on the mental lexicon. It is written in an accessible and often humorous and light-hearted way but covers all the most serious issues connected with how the mind stores and processes vocabulary. It not only covers the linguistic aspects of the mental lexicon but also looks at the role of the human brain in language. It is essential reading for anyone interested in the mental lexicon.

Clark, E. V. 2016. *First Language Acquisition*. Third edition. Cambridge: Cambridge University Press.
Eve Clark's book takes the reader through all the stages of language acquisition, from babies' first sounds to the maturing child's ability to use language skilfully and meaningfully. It shows how children acquire language through conversation and interaction. It is written in an accessible style and covers aspects of language, psychology, and cognitive development.

Schmitt, N. (ed.) 2004. *Formulaic Sequences*. Amsterdam: John Benjamins.
Norbert Schmitt is one of the foremost scholars in the field of second-language vocabulary acquisition. In this book, he brings together his own research and research by others mentioned in this chapter, including Paul Nation and Alison Wray. The chapters cover aspects such as corpus investigation of formulaic chunks, the processing of chunks of various kinds, and how learners acquire them.

VOCABULARY IN ACTION

WORDS OUT THERE

Chapter 5 was about words in the mind, the mental lexicon. This chapter is about words in the world, English vocabulary in society, or vocabulary 'out there'. But just as we have seen in previous chapters, not only is vocabulary complex in terms of linguistic forms or in terms of the invisible workings of the mental lexicon, it is also complex in terms of its many social roles. We are surrounded by vocabulary in our daily lives, in speaking, listening, reading, and writing, in books, newspapers, magazines, letters, forms, and other paper documents, on the internet in websites, blogs, chat rooms, and social media postings, on radio and TV, in films and video clips, in classrooms and school textbooks, in public signs and advertisements (the **linguistic landscape**), in poetry and the dramatic arts, and in word games and puzzles. The list is endless. This chapter will sample just some of the many contexts.

One tension that arises in attempting to nail down the social identity of English vocabulary is that, on the one hand, a great deal of effort has been dedicated to recording and preserving the vocabulary but on the other hand the vocabulary is constantly shifting and changing, adapting itself to society. Vocabulary is more like quicksand than solid rock, and it is this tension between convention and stability, creativity, and change that we explore in this final chapter. We start with dictionaries. Printed dictionaries try to take a snapshot of the quicksand, to freeze it in time on paper, but the shifting sands refuse to stand still, and dictionaries do not escape public debate and controversy. They are social artefacts.

DOI: 10.4324/9781003284611-7

LANGUAGE SNAPSHOTS

HARD WORDS

In Chapter 2, we looked at the first dictionary devoted entirely to English (i.e., a monolingual one, not one for translation), which was published in 1604. It may look now like a dull, archaic volume, but it tells us a lot about the role of vocabulary in early seventeenth-century educated English society. It had the title *Table Alphabeticall* and was compiled by Robert Cawdrey (see p. 43). It consists of an alphabetical list of close to 3,000 words with synonyms or a very brief definition for each headword. However, even more illuminating than the choice of words included are Cawdrey's views on the social status of English vocabulary at that time. Cawdrey labelled the dictionary as a book of 'hard' words, the idea being to elevate the knowledge of its users by introducing them to correct and proper usage of Hebrew-, Greek-, Latin-, and French-based words and to counteract the importing of foreign words and fancy vocabulary, which he felt was often used simply for effect. At that time, English was an expanding language in terms of new vocabulary in science and scholarship. At the same time, Britain was expanding its trade and imperial ambitions around the world, the result of which was that the language burst its local bounds and, ultimately, became the world language we know today. Cawdrey's dictionary was more than just a record: it was an attempt at social engineering.

INFORMATION ADD-ON

Here are some entries from the letter G in Cawdrey's *Table Alphabeti-call*. They are very different from modern dictionary entries which give detailed definitions and examples of usage. They look more like a thesaurus, giving synonyms and related expressions. Notice how modern spellings had not yet become completely fixed.

Gratifie – to pleasure, or doo a good turne in way of thankfulness
Gratis – freely, without desert [*desert* = without deserving any recompense]
Gratitude – thankfulness
Gratulate – to be glad for another's sake [compare modern *congratulate*]

(Examples from Cawdrey 1604/1966)

There have been many English dictionaries published since 1604, but here we need only note that dictionaries are not neutral artefacts or objective archives of the vocabulary. Dictionaries reflect not only words in circulation when they were compiled, but also the cultures and social preoccupations of their time and are testimonies of the choices lexicographers make in deciding what to include and what to exclude.

NOT IN FRONT OF THE CHILDREN

In the decade preceding the publication of this book, controversy raged online and in the press in the English-speaking world over the updating of a dictionary for youngsters published by Oxford University Press. New editions of the dictionary had removed a number of words related to the natural world which had featured in previous editions, including *acorn, bluebell, cygnet, dandelion, heron, otter, pasture,* and *raven.* The controversy made headlines in 2017, when 53,000 people signed a petition to reinstate the lost words.[1] The petition later grew to 200,000 signatures. Well-known writers were up in arms. Children from a primary school on Vancouver Island, Canada, joined in the protest and complained to the Oxford press (see the Canadian Broadcasting Corporation report).[2] In place of the nature words, the publisher had added new entries, including words such as *blog, broadband, voicemail, chat room,* and *celebrity.*

REFLECTION POINT

As languages change, dictionaries change; old words drop out, new words come in. In an urbanized society, is it justifiable to exclude unfamiliar words from the natural world which children might want or need to look up, for the sake of including new words they may already be fully familiar with through their use of technology?

Oxford University Press defends its choice of words for its dictionaries on the basis that its lexicographers consult corpora as objective evidence of the current state of the language; in the case of the children's dictionary, a special children's corpus was used.

Should dictionaries simply record the vocabulary or do more, and give advice and warnings on its use? One North American reviewer, in defence of the controversial Oxford children's dictionary, reminded readers of the *Washington Post* that the celebrated *Webster's Third New International Dictionary* abandoned the **prescriptive** tradition (advising users how to use words correctly) for a more **descriptive** approach in its new 1961 edition (Huler 2018). *Descriptive* means recording the vocabulary as it is, rather than how we might think or wish it to be, and that is where corpora come into their own (see below).

Printed editions of dictionaries tend to be snapshots of the language at the time they are written, with the exception of historical dictionaries. Online dictionaries have the advantage of being able to be updated very quickly. The *Oxford English Dictionary* (OED) online, for example, recorded 700 new entries and senses and additions and revisions in just the three months up to June 2021.[3] Meanwhile, the *Merriam-Webster* online *Word-O-Meter* records real-time statistics on what words people are looking up in the dictionary at any given moment, providing a fascinating window on the public's encounters with vocabulary and the lexical information they are seeking.[4] English dictionaries have come a long way since the days of hefty volumes languishing on bookshelves; they now form the basis of spell-checkers and thesauruses in computer word processing and predictive text programmes, and online dictionaries usually include audio clips for pronunciation, sometimes in more than one variety of English. Nonetheless, they are still tied to their cultural environment and their time.

LETTING THE MACHINE DECIDE: CORPORA

QUIZZING THE DATA

In using software to analyse corpora, we hand over the most time-consuming tasks of describing English vocabulary to the machine, as we saw in the discussion of corpora in Chapter 1. If we collect enough data and base our data collection on questions which we seek answers to, we can illuminate aspects of the role of vocabulary in our social activity in a more objective way than that which our intuitions permit. Some of the questions about vocabulary which corpora can help us to answer are:

- Do different dialects and varieties of English have words and expressions that significantly distinguish them from one another?
- How rapidly is the vocabulary changing? What types of changes are involved?
- How do specialist domains distinguish themselves in terms of their vocabulary?
- What can corpora tell us about vocabulary differences among populations in relation, for example, to age, social class, culture, etc.?
- How far do corpora offer evidence of the reliability of the theoretical models of vocabulary we have discussed in earlier chapters (e.g., collocation, synonymy, hyponymy, metonymy, and idiomaticity)?

In all these questions, the computer has no prejudices, no axe to grind; it simply counts the data put into it in ways that can provide useful statistical output and reveal patterns of use. At the click of a mouse, the computer can do what would take hundreds of hours of human labour and manual counting and observation to accomplish. It can answer many of the questions we set it but can also throw up surprises and provide insights and facts about vocabulary that might never have occurred to us. Of course, any corpus is only as good as the data entered into it, and many more questions than those listed above can, and have been, asked of corpora to further our understanding of vocabulary. In the limited space of this 'basics' book, we can tackle just a few.

EXCHANGING A FEW WORDS

The discussion in Chapter 3 of synonymy, antonymy, and hyponymy was based on the exploration of sense relations, mostly at a theoretical, model-building level. But why should English have near-synonyms, superordinate terms, antonyms, etc.? We organize the world conceptually into classes of things, and perceiving similarities and contrasts between things ensures our mental sanity and serves practical purposes, but we also interact with our fellow human beings, and it is there that we can observe some interesting aspects of the systems of meanings and sense relations we seem to carry around in our heads. They enable us to refer to shared worlds and to converge on ways of understanding our experiences.

In the Spoken BNC2014, a search for significant collocations of *beautiful* yields *lovely* and *stunning* among the top 15 collocates. Why should a word collocate with its own synonyms in ordinary conversation? One reason is that speakers need to project not just what a word means but what *they mean by* that word, how they want to be understood, in other words, pragmatic meaning. Consider this example:

<S0564> *Lake Bled it was* **nice** *it was* **lovely** *and we were we didn't have a lot of money that year so we went there cos it was er so much cheaper*
<S0543> *mm* <S0565> <*overlap*> *mm*
<S0564> *and really loved it didn't we?*
<S0565> *it was* **beautiful** *yeah*
<S0564> **beautiful**
<S0565> <*overlap*> *mm yeah* **lovely**
<S0543> *mm*
<S0564> **lovely** *atmosphere* **lovely**

(Spoken BNC2014 SNYC)

The adjectives in bold are all concerned with evaluating a holiday in Lake Bled (Slovenia). Speaker 0564 uses *nice, lovely, beautiful,* and then *lovely* again twice. Speaker 065 uses *beautiful* then *lovely.* Are these just boring speakers with a limited vocabulary? That would be a most unfair conclusion. In fact, repetition of words and the interspersion of near-synonyms by the same speaker or across different speakers is a common feature of all conversation. It enables people to negotiate meaning. Common, everyday words have conventional agreed meanings in a general but somewhat fuzzy sense, and those meanings can change over time, but what really matters is what speakers do with words and what they intend to mean by their words, their pragmatic meanings, and how these converge or diverge.

Most conversation is collaborative and convergent, and the back-and-forth exchanges of vocabulary are central to the efforts speakers make to converge wherever they can. Synonyms do not pre-exist in language as if carved in stone; they are created and moulded over time by hundreds of thousands of users. The interplay of words in the conversation extract above points to the **emergent** nature of meaning. Meanings are never fixed or finalized but are always in process. For example, in the OED, fifteenth- and sixteenth-century uses of the adjective *amazing* show it meaning 'confusing, terrifying and awful', in other words, a negative connotation. Seventeenth-century examples and onward show it with a positive meaning of 'great surprise and wonder' and by the twentieth century and today it has come to mean *excellent*. This transition of *amazing* from synonymy to antonymy in relation to *terrible* and from antonymy to synonymy in relation to *excellent* did not happen by government decree but by real people using the words in real situations. There is no guarantee that *amazing* will keep its present connotations 10, 20, or more years from now.

LET'S NOT GO INTO DETAIL

Beyond the grammar-dominated most frequent 100 spoken items where we see pronouns, prepositions, determiners, and so on, we find that the next 165 items in the spoken list capture more and more lexical words. These still have high frequencies ranging from over 11,000 occurrences at the top end to 3,000 at the lower end, a convenient cut-off point for our present purposes. The 165 items contain words which often turn out to be parts of chunks that are typical of conversational speech. Here is a sample from the list:

sort, only, something, anything, fact, everything, somebody

If we let the software run a collocational analysis on these words, we find significant collocates that immediately give us the flavour of conversation. The single words and their collocates now become visible as high-frequency chunks:

sort of, that sort of thing, the only thing is, something like that, or anything, in (actual) fact, and everything, somebody else

Several of these are examples of vague language expressions which are characteristic of informal speaking. The next two examples show them in action:

> [the speaker is describing the first day of a new job on a building site. 'Him' is a friend of the speaker's father]
>
> *And er I got going with that, carting bricks and timber **and all that sort of thing** for him*

(BNC 1994 FY1)

> *I'll have ham or chicken roll or **something like that**.*

(BNC 1994 KBW)

Bricks and *timber* are immediately associated in the speaker's and listener's mind with the construction industry; *ham* and *chicken* are typical fillings for sandwiches and bread rolls. In each of these examples, the speaker chooses two **exemplars** and then projects the rest of the lexical field that they belong to, using a vague expression, which obviates the need to tiresomely list in detail everything on a building site or all possible sandwich fillings. Exemplars are the 'best examples', the most immediate items that speakers associate with a class of people or things. There is a direct link here with the discussion in Chapter 3 of hyponymy and stereotypes.

Vocabulary theories and models should be judged by the extent to which we can observe them functioning in our social lives as well as pondering their place in the invisible world of the mental lexicon. In this case, vague language expressions put flesh on the bones of the notions of hyponymy and salience of meaning, as well demonstrating our ability to create shortcuts to the mental lexicon and the 'shared mental space' of social interaction. Figure 6.1 is a good example: the reader is invited to 'fill in' the vague reference of 'and more' – the shop does not need to list everything it sells but can rely on the exemplars to trigger more co-hyponyms and other related items.

Vague language expressions permeate our social life, not just in chats between friends. My co-researchers Anne O'Keeffe and Steve Walsh and I investigated spoken academic language and were surprised at just how many times academics use vague expressions – perhaps we were expecting razor-like precision in academic

Figure 6.1 Vague language: *And more* ... Image © Michael McCarthy. Sign reproduced by kind permission.

language – yet it is clear that vague expressions are a very economical way of referring to shared concepts and linking new ideas to existing academic knowledge (see Walsh *et al.* 2008). The linguist Joan Cutting edited a volume of papers on vague expressions which showed their use in, among other contexts, talk among colleagues in the workplace, in mathematics classrooms, in healthcare and courtrooms, and in several varieties of English, including British, Irish, American, Hong Kong, and New Zealand (Cutting 2007).

IN THEORY AND IN PRACTICE

Formal writing has its own distinctive vocabulary, especially when it comes to linking words and expressions. These are used to express logical connections between ideas. In my book on grammar in this *Basics* series, I showed how linking expressions such as *subsequently*, *consequently*, and *nonetheless* were many times more frequent in the written texts of the BNC 1994 than in its spoken transcripts (McCarthy 2021b: 52). Figure 6.2 shows some examples of differences in frequency in writing and speaking in the BNC 1994 in the use of

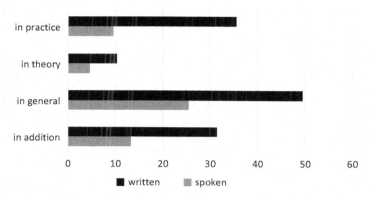

Figure 6.2 Discourse markers in writing and speaking.

discourse-marking expressions (used to organize or express the writer's/speaker's stance towards the message) beginning with *in*. Although our examples of linking expressions and discourse markers are also heard in formal speaking, such as lectures, their frequency in formal writing is far greater than in everyday conversation.

Formal writing at one end of the scale and informal speaking at the other have overlapping but distinct vocabularies which give them their 'fingerprint' or 'DNA'. But note that these are ends of a scale. In between, there exists a wide range of types of writing which are more like speaking, and types of speaking which are more like writing. Texting, social media posting, blogs, emails, and other e-language have blurred the distinction between speaking and writing even more.

REFLECTION POINT

Consider this exchange between me and a good friend trying to arrange to meet to rehearse music for a concert. Is it a transcript of a face-to-face conversation or is it a series of text messages bouncing back and forth on our phones? What makes it possible to decide one way or the other?

ME: We're thinking Wednesday 4pm our place

FRIEND: Should be okay. What is the date of the concert?

ME: Saturday 3rd July at 7pm

FRIEND: Thanks

WINDOWS ON CULTURE

In Chapter 3, we saw how the different frequencies of cooking verbs in the BNC 1994 told us much about the kinds of activities people typically engage in when preparing food. Another point to emerge from the discussion of meaning was that not all words that belong to the same lexical set are equal. Some are more salient than others; some tend to be seen as prototypes for their class. Corpora consistently show us that words in lexical sets are rarely equal in terms of their frequency of use. Figure 6.3 shows the relative frequency of the names of the days of the week in the 11.5 million words of the Spoken BNC 2014.

We see a week which appears to be focused on the weekend, with the first part of the week, especially Tuesday, a seemingly lower priority topic of conversation. This is hardly surprising given the fact that people look forward to the weekend and often plan their social life around those days, with Friday marking the end of the working week in western cultures. And after the weekend, people talk about what they did on Friday, Saturday, and Sunday. Different cultures and religions may have a different pattern of the week and the weekend. The corpus is providing a window onto culture as well as revealing that lexical sets typically do not contain words of equal frequency or salience. A similar pattern of unequal frequencies will be found with

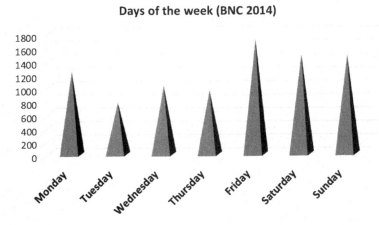

Figure 6.3 Frequencies of days of the week.

sets such as colour terms and seasons of the year, as well as the uneven frequencies in the names of the parts of the human body arising from their different idiom-proneness (see Chapter 4).

WORDS ON THE MOVE

NAUGHTY BUT NICE

As we have argued in this book, vocabulary never stands still. We have seen how many new words lexicographers have to contend with every year in deciding what to put into their dictionaries. New words come in; old words drop out. We saw in Chapter 1 how rapid technology changes can result in words having a relatively short life before they fade away (e.g., *telex, camcorder, pager*). Other changes are more subtle: *railway station* is fast giving way to *train station* in British English (BrE), while American *airplane* is now increasingly heard instead of *aeroplane*. Words can survive by changing their meaning to adapt to social developments. For example, 400 years ago, the verb *to advertise* meant to notify or warn someone in a rather serious way. Nowadays, it means to attract people's attention to something in order that they will buy, participate, etc. *Random*, which used to be confined to the world of statistics, meaning 'occurring by chance', has now come also to mean 'strange or odd'. A *gig* was once a horse-drawn vehicle; in the twentieth century, it acquired its meaning of an engagement for a musician or performer. Other words which have shifted their meaning over the centuries include *naughty* (originally 'possessing nothing', then morally bad, wicked, or violent, nowadays disobedient, mischievous), and *nice* (originally stupid or ignorant – compare Spanish *necio* – then precise or rigorous, as in *a nice point*, nowadays pleasant or attractive). Both words are in partnership in the current expression *naughty but nice* referring to something that is bad for us but pleasurable at the same time.

A NOTICEABLE UPTICK

English vocabulary embraces a plethora of phrasal verbs and related expressions. These are often informal substitutes for more formal-sounding words of Greek, Latin, or French origin, and their noticeable use in the media and public life is a sign of a general move towards informality in English-speaking societies and away from the old, scholastic tradition of adhering to Greek- and Latin-inspired words. Recent additions to the vocabulary of BrE, with their more formal alternatives, include:

> *chill out* (relax, remain calm), *badge in/out* (use an electronic badge to enter/leave secure locations), call *out* (challenge, expose wrongdoing), *shout out/a shout-out* (thank, congratulate or praise), *double down on* (strengthen, emphasise), *mask up* (don a mask), *push back* (resist, challenge, counter), *dial down* (reduce intensity), *reach out* (contact), *levelling up* (improving equality of opportunity), *uptick* (increase, rise), *onboarding* (welcoming and integrating a new employee/colleague)

All these are attested and discussed by members of the Facebook Language Observatory Group (LOG), who post examples of any language use that they find new or unfamiliar. Most have entered BrE from North American English (AmE), especially in the social media and journalistic world. AmE influence can also be seen in the addition of particles to verbs which traditionally in BrE needed no particle, as in *Listen up! Wait up!* The American economist Diane Swonk, discussing Federal interest rate cuts on BBC radio in October 2019, used the following phrasal expressions, all in the space of an interview of just a couple of minutes:

> the pushback and the fatigue of cutting rates… a rollback in tariffs… the pullback in investment… a pullback in hiring… the consumer pulled back in the height of the holiday season… a pullback in spending… consumers pulled back on discretionary spending

For further examples and a discussion, see Chapter 9 of my book on innovations and challenges in grammar (McCarthy 2021a). The economist's use of the phrasal expressions above can also be seen as elements of a special vocabulary, a badge of identity as a member of her professional community.

INFORMATION ADD-ON

Google Ngram Viewer enables the user to track changes in the frequency of a word or phrase over time. Here we see how the phrasal verb *chill out* increased in frequency in BrE over the period 1980–2018 (Figure 6.4).

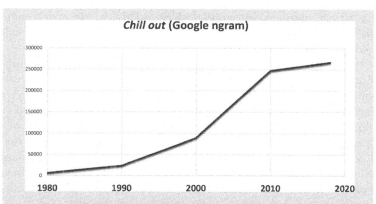

Figure 6.4 Chill out in British English 1980–2018. (http://books.google.com/ngrams)

SHOWING YOUR AGE

Another force for change in vocabulary comes with the birth of each new generation. Some words and expressions are used more by older speakers; some are favoured by younger speakers. Items chosen can be seen as tokens of membership of different age groups. Earlier, we mentioned the shift in meaning of *random*, from being associated with events happening by chance to meaning 'strange' or 'odd'. The *BNC lab* website enables users to see, among other things, how any item in the spoken BNC corpora of 1994 and 2014 is distributed across the two corpora and across different age groups (Brezina *et al.* 2018). *Random* shows a distinct clustering of use in the younger generation of late teenagers and 20–40 year olds and is ten times more frequent in the 2014 corpus than in the 1994 version. The 1994 examples have technical terms such as *at random, random access,* and *random error* as prominent collocates, while the 2014 examples show collocations such as *random person/people/stuff/strangers,* reflecting the shift in meaning. Web searches for young people's slang words in 2022 yielded, among others, *dope* (= cool, great, awesome) and *salty* (= angry, upset). New uses of words may come and go, but some have staying power and will remain in the usage of age groups as they mature and grow older. The use of *gear* as a positive adjective by celebrities such as the Beatles in the 1960s has all but vanished, yet words such as *cool* and *awesome*, so trendy amongst the young 30–40 years ago have now become almost bland and normal.

Fiona Farr and Bróna Murphy, two scholars who research Irish English, studied the use of chunks in a corpus of informal conversations recorded in Ireland (Farr and Murphy 2009). They were interested in age and gender differences in the use of religious expressions (expressions involving words such as *God, Lord, Jesus, Christ, devil*) in non-religious contexts. Using a sub-corpus of the Limerick Corpus of Irish English consisting of conversations among women in three age groups (20, 40, and 70–80 years old), they found that there was a difference in the distribution of the vocabulary in the three groups. Chunks such as *God almighty, God above,* and *Glory be to God* were more commonly used among the older speakers, and far less so among the youngest. This is put down to changes in Irish society as regards the erstwhile revered status of religion. Farr and Murphy also noted gender differences, showing the complexity of the relationship between age, gender, context, and social change in the makeup of a national vocabulary.

MAPPING ENGLISH VOCABULARY

VARIETIES

English exists as many different, independent varieties around the world beyond the BrE variety that most of this book is based around. Each of these world Englishes has its own characteristics of pronunciation, grammar, and vocabulary, most of which are now well-documented. There are several ways in which world varieties of English have evolved. One factor in the past was distance and isolation from the original motherland. Forms of English taken to North America and Australia, for example, in the early days of colonization often persisted in relatively isolated communities, and the vocabulary evolved there and in its British homeland in different ways. One linguist describes the situation thus:

> The early American settlers were faced with radically new experiences and objects, and to meet their needs to designate these, they either borrowed or coined new words. By the eighteenth century such

"Americanisms" abounded, and lexicographers, most notably the patriotic Noah Webster, began to record and emphasize the lexical distinctiveness of American English — it is interesting to see that this "linguistic declaration of independence" followed the political separation of the United States from her British mother country.

(Schneider 2009: 60)

Another factor was the presence of the languages of other colonizing powers, traders, and immigrants. In Canada, for example, French words influenced the English of regions such as Quebec. The Canadian scholar Charles Boberg notes the example of *dépanneur* (often shortened to *dep*) to refer to what in Britain might be a corner shop selling newspapers, tobacco products, snacks, etc., while a pizza with multiple toppings is called *all dressed*, a translation of the French *toute garnie* (Boberg 2005).

REFLECTION POINT

Although North American English has its origins in a variety forged by colonizers, traders, and immigrants, nowadays it has, in its turn, become the variety of English that has the greatest influence in the world, especially in popular culture and on the internet. Consider your own variety of English or any other language you know and the extent to which its vocabulary is subject to American influences, whether it be new words or the spelling/pronunciation of existing ones.

By far the most significant influence on the development of varieties of English in many parts of the world was **language contact**, where English as the incoming, colonizing language came into contact with local languages through administration, trade, education, social relationships, etc., resulting in mutual influence. For example, the proximity of Latin America and contact with Spanish in the southern parts of the United States has given rise to a Hispanic-influenced English (Schneider 2009: 65). In East Asia, Hong Kong English is marked by code-mixing of Cantonese chunks in English conversation (Wong 2017: ch5). Malaysian English developed out of a complex pool of language contact between English, Malay,

Chinese, Indian, Arabic, and indigenous languages. Although the official national language, Bahasa Malaysia, has been strongly promoted in education and public life over the years, English has remained an important language and the lexicon of colloquial Malaysian English has distinct characteristics. An article by Azira Hashim and Gerhard Leitner lists many words used in Malaysian English that originated in the languages of the different ethnicities, religions, and cultures that make up modern Malaysia. These include:

Salam (Arabic greeting)
Haram (Arabic: forbidden by the laws of Islam)
Chit (Indian: official note)
Bomoh (Malay: traditional healer)
(Hashim and Leitner 2011: 556–558)

Along with words like *kampong* (village) and *hawker* (street food seller), as well as names of local dishes and food items, these and many other words commonly heard in colloquial Malaysian English became part of my normal, everyday vocabulary when I lived there in the early 1980s, and I very quickly stopped thinking of them as anything other than local English. As one study puts it:

> The local variety of English is seen as a versatile variety that is viable for effective communication and not as a distortion of the English language. It is used to mark identity and solidarity among Malaysians.
> (Pillai and Ong 2018: 150)

Fiji, where English is an official language, is another example of multiple language contact which has influenced the lexicon of the local variety of English. Jan Tent lists examples of Fiji English vocabulary and concludes that 'Fiji English is as distinctive as that of any other post-colonial variety of English' (Tent 2001: 217). Idioms and fixed expressions with their origin in indigenous language contact also identify distinct varieties, for example, in Nigerian English, as discussed by Umar (2019).

In its role as a supra-national language and in the era of instant global communication, varieties are no longer isolated. The lexicon of world English has been influenced not only by particular geographical varieties but also by the emergence of online registers which utilize vocabulary from a wide range of world Englishes, not just dominant varieties such as BrE or AmE (see Bohmann 2019: ch2 for a discussion).

INFORMATION ADD-ON

English is an official language in many countries around the world. On the African continent, the following countries use English, and distinct varieties involving local vocabularies have evolved across the continent.

Botswana, Cameroon, Eswatin, Gambia, Ghana, Kenya, Lesotho, Liberia, Malawi, Namibia, Nigeria, Rwanda, South Africa, South Sudan, Sudan, Tanzania, Uganda, Zambia, Zimbabwe

The Englishes of the different countries and regions of the world are covered in detail in Cheshire (1991).

DIFFERENT VOICES: DIALECTS AND SOCIOLECTS

The previous section considered English around the world and the significance of vocabulary in contributing to the identity of world English varieties. Yet each of those varieties will also contain internal variation: AmE, the shorthand for 'American English', embraces the English of a vast country, the USA, and is often used to include Canada. Within those countries, we will find different accents, differences in grammar, and different vocabulary, in other words, different dialects. **Dialects** are distinct ways of using a language based on regional or local differences. For example, during the coronavirus pandemic of 2020, vaccines were developed to counter the devastating effects of the virus. Getting vaccinated was known as getting a *shot* in AmE, a *jab* in England and a *jag* in Scotland – three different words current in three regions of the English-speaking world.

Sometimes, dialectal differences can be on quite a small scale. Great Britain is a relatively small geographical area yet dialect differences in terms of vocabulary can be quite marked even over short distances. In different parts of England, a narrow passage between buildings may be called an *alley*, a *snicket*, or a *ginnel*. The BBC's *Bitesize* educational web pages have more examples of these and other words from around the UK.[5] If you know about dialects in the UK, you will be aware of terms such as *Geordie* (the style of speaking in parts of Northeast England), *Scouse* (the dialect of the Liverpool region), and *Cockney* (a London dialect). In terms of vocabulary, dialect identity is often marked by different pronunciations of the same word or different words and expressions applied to the same meaning. The USA has marked dialect differences between the English of its northern and southern states and between its major cities; Ireland has a dialectal division between its northern province and the southern ones, while its cities (Cork, Dublin, Belfast) have noticeable differences in pronunciation and vocabulary (Figure 6.5).

REFLECTION POINT

One main feature of dialects is the way words are pronounced. In the county of Cambridgeshire, UK, where I live, the /juː/ sound, as in *you* in standard BrE *music, news, bugle, computer, human,* is pronounced as /uː/, as in *too*, so we hear /'muːzɪk/, /nuːz/, /'buːgəl/, /kəmˈpuːtə/, /ˈhuːmən/.

Consider any pronunciation differences from standard BrE in the vocabulary of your variety of English or local dialect, or any other variety or dialect you are familiar with.

Figure 6.5 Bugle or boogle? © Jake Tebbit 2022.

However, not all differences in vocabulary can be put down to geography. Australian English, for example, is seen to be more greatly differentiated along sociolinguistic lines than geographical differences, even though it originally grew out of different English dialects. Gregory Guy says of Australian English: 'Internally it shows a relative absence of geographic differentiation combined with a striking presence of social differentiation' (Guy 1991: 224). Variations based on social groups are called **sociolects**, which may be based on social class, age (see above), or other social group identities. Often, speakers of sociolects and dialects are looked down upon as inferior to speakers of standard, officially sanctioned forms of the language as used in education, broadcasting, and public life. To dismiss social and geographical vocabulary differences as inferior or incorrect is unjustified, and, as the dialect scholars Hughes and Trudgill (1979: 12) put it the notion of 'correctness' in accents and dialects is 'an irrelevance'. Dialects and sociolects are as well-formed and as communicative as any standard language, are a core part of people's identities, and serve to create and maintain social cohesion. In many cases, they are precious links with lost rural and industrial pasts. What may be important in education is to help children to understand that in their social lives, there will be choices to make as to whether to use standard forms or dialect/sociolect vocabulary, depending on the situation, who they are talking to, and so on.

INFORMATION ADD-ON

Here are some words from colloquial Australian English. Note the preference for the 'diminutive' effect of the -y/-ie ending. Such vocabulary expresses informality, friendliness, and social bonding.

arvo (afternoon), *barbie* (barbecue), *footy* (football), *sunnies* (sunglasses), *rellies* (relatives), *brekkie* (breakfast)

Research suggests that younger age groups have particular preferences in using informal diminutives, for example, for technical items such as *lappy* (laptop) and *webby* (webcam). See the discussion on the Australian Geographic website.[6]

SPECIAL VOCABULARIES

Professional communities can manifest their identities through their use of vocabulary. Academic discourse, for example, has scientific and technical terms which are rare or seldom heard in general, everyday language. Terms used in this book, for example, *collocation, hyponymy, denotation, morpheme, multi-word unit,* and *mental lexicon,* are not part of most people's daily usage. Such special terms become the linguistic fingerprint of professional groups.

As an example of this 'fingerprinting' of specialist discourse, let's consider the results of a keyword analysis of the British Academic Written English (BAWE) corpus.[7] BAWE consists of around 3,000 university student assignments, a total of 6.5 million words taken from four general disciplinary areas (Arts and Humanities, Social Sciences, Life Sciences, and Physical Sciences). If we measure BAWE against a benchmark of a sub-corpus of general books in the BNC 1994, we find some illustrative examples in the top 20 lemmas. Table 6.1 shows a selection and relevant collocations and/or chunks (chunks are shown in bold).

Although any one of these key lemmas may occur in everyday, non-academic writing, the computer has identified them as being particularly significant in academic contexts, and their collocations and chunks immediately recreate the tone of academic discourse. For example, the chunk *in terms of,* which roughly means 'in relation to', is strongly linked with processes of explaining, measuring, and describing; *depending on* is used in contexts where variation is the result of factors which will be listed/discussed. Both chunks serve core academic and intellectual activity.

Special vocabularies have developed in a range of professional domains, for example, business English, legal English, the English

Table 6.1 Sample of key lemmas from BAWE.

Item	Collocations/Chunks
according	vary, varies, classified **according to**
terms	explained, expressed, measured, described **in terms of**
including	several, various, many, factors, variety, characteristics, features
regarding	information, debate, discussion, questions, issues, opinions
depending	vary, varies **depending on** whether
concerning	information, understanding, issues, debate

of religious ritual, journalism, and the mass media. Journalists and broadcasters often use terms which, although understood by their audiences, would be unlikely to be used by them in everyday conversation, for example, *ahead of* [before] *tomorrow's meeting of European leaders, at the top of the hour, at the top of the programme, breaking news, we'll keep you across* [up to date with] *that story, our sister station* [radio], and so on. Financial services also have their special vocabulary, which can sometimes come over as jargon (special vocabulary which has become a convenient shorthand for people who work together but challenging for outsiders). In this case, the intricate world of finance has generated a necessary, if difficult to process, set of terms. Here are some examples of communications from a financial adviser to a client (it should be added that this particular adviser is always kindly on hand to explain everything in lay terms!):

> This note has annual observation dates and if the terms have been met, based on the S&P 500 and the Eurostoxx 50 indices ("the indices"), it matures and pays its return of 9.85% per annum. If the terms are not met, the note continues to the next annual observation date, until it matures after seven years.
> Typically this type of note would have 250–300% upside. This is an institutional product that we have launched on a bespoke basis with the objective of taking advantage of a spike in volatility generally ...
>
> (Reproduced by kind permission)

None of the words in these extracts, apart from the name Eurostxx 50, is a word I have never seen before, yet I struggle to understand the messages, mostly because of the technical collocations (*annual observation dates, 250–300% upside, a spike in volatility*, etc.).

WORDS AND THE IMAGINATION

FLOUTING CONVENTIONS

At any given point in time, we can view the vocabulary of English as a relatively stable social compact affirmed by its users – we agree on what the acceptable words and expressions of English are in our social, regional, national, or global identities at that time. We agree on the notion of a 'standard' vocabulary which will serve education, journalism, and public life in general. With regard to individual words, we more or less agree on how to pronounce them, how to spell them, what their denotations and connotations are, how their meanings relate to one another in lexical sets, how they collocate and form chunks, what grammatical classes they belong to, and how formal or informal, technical or non-technical they are. Without such an underlying agreement, communication would be hazardous and would amount to no more than continuous guesswork with potentially disastrous consequences.

However, we are also creative and use our imagination. In the worlds of poetry, drama, journalism, advertising, humour, and entertainment, vocabulary is a resource for creating new forms and new meanings, for re-shaping the old, agreed forms and meanings into messages that appeal to the eye and the ear, and which can touch our emotions, passions, moods, and sensitivities and kindle new sparks of original and innovative thoughts in our minds. We do not communicate only through dull conventionality.

OLD WORDS, NEW MEANINGS

In creative uses of vocabulary, we can see principles discussed in the earlier chapters of this book in action. The exploitation of collocational norms is characteristic of poetry. The Welsh poet, Dylan Thomas, in his famous work for radio, *Under Milk Wood*, refers to the night as *bible-black* and to the sea as *sloeblack* and *crowblack*. These are unusual collocations for the colour black, more typically associated with expressions such as *pitch black* or *jet black*, both of which are among the top 15 collocates of *black* in the BNC 1994.

Hyponymy and lexical set membership is also open to exploitation. The following lines from a poem by the contemporary British poet James Womack combine items from different lexical sets in unusual ways. The poet is lamenting the ageing process and the effects of age on his skin:

> My complexion was a mixture of snow and roses,
> and now it is meltwater and lilies, linen and paper,
> pale as the vampire death I need to come and take me.
>
> (Womak 2020: 19; reproduced by kind permission)

Snow and *meltwater* (lexical field: weather phenomena) and *roses* and *lilies* (lexical field: flowers) are mixed together (*snow* with *roses*; *meltwater* with *lilies*), as are *linen* and *paper*, two kinds of material from different sets of co-hyponyms. At the same time, there is a suggested antonymy between the beauty of snow and the chilling disintegration of meltwater, between the redness of roses and the pallor of lilies, linen and paper. The *pale vampire* is both a reference to the mythical, deathly whiteness of a vampire's face surrounded by the darkness in which the vampire prowls and an oblique echo of James Joyce's *Ulysses*, which includes reference to a *pale vampire* in one of its scenes (see the discussion in Martin 1986). Using vocabulary in this way, echoing the words from another text to stimulate images, characters, or ideas from another text, is an example of **intertextuality**. Intertextuality is a resource often used in headline writing and advertising. The *New Scientist* magazine in 2022 published an article on how to grow strawberries successfully. The headline was *Strawberry yields forever*, a punning reference to the Beatles' song of 1967, *Strawberry Fields Forever* (Wilson 2022). References like these depend on cultural links which uses of vocabulary can forge and may not necessarily be language-wide but depend on a degree of local or in-group shared knowledge. If you have not read James Joyce or are not familiar with Beatles songs, the allusions may be lost on you.

FOOD FOR THOUGHT

Advertisements serve a wide range of functions in society. As the linguist Guy Cook puts it, as well as trying to sell products, advertisements may 'amuse, inform, misinform, worry or warn' (Cook 2001: 10). He mentions the importance of connotation and metaphor in the use of words in advertising (p.12). Another aspect of vocabulary which is relevant to advertising is word association, which we discussed in Chapter 5 in relation to the mental lexicon. There are a number of marketing techniques which attempt to get at what consumers find attractive in products so that they can be advertised more effectively; exploiting word association is one of them. Journals devoted to marketing and advertising abound in investigations of consumer preferences based on word association experiments. For instance, Guerrero *et al.* (2010), in a major study across different European regions, tested people's associations with the word *traditional* as applied to food products. They found a tendency among southern European consumers to associate *traditional* with heritage, culture, and history, while northern European consumers associated the word more with convenience and health. Other associations with *traditional* included *variety, origin, simplicity,* and *special occasions.* Once again, we see the more abstract and psychological aspects of vocabulary study in action in the world, this time with economic and commercial consequences.

The tension between idiomatic and literal meaning is often creatively exploited, as in the headline to an article about the advent of electrically powered aeroplanes: *Electric aviation is no flight of fancy;*[8] *a flight of fancy* is an idiomatic compound meaning an idea that is very creative but not realistic or practical. Other types of chunks are also exploited, for example, an advertisement to attract tourists to the Isle of Man (an island between Britain and Ireland) boasts that it is just *a hop, skip and a ferry ride away*[9] – an allusion to the trinomial expression *just a hop, skip and a jump,* meaning that a place is nearby and easily reached.

REFLECTION POINT

What aspects of vocabulary discussed in earlier chapters in this book are exploited in the following advertising slogans and headlines?

Why not have your cake and eat it?
You can bank on us to take care of your finances
Sole searching – we seek out the most comfortable men's shoes
Transport Minister takes voters for a ride
Yule love our Christmas puddings
Son-rise: how George made it to the top with his father's help.
Paws for thought: understanding cats

HAVING A LAUGH

Advertising often exploits humour, and a great deal of English language humour depends on manipulating the vocabulary in some way. This could be, for example, basing an advertisement on homophones, as in the headline in a British newspaper magazine supplement, *The Ruff Guide,*[10] to draw attention to an article about different breeds of dogs; *ruff* imitates the bark of a dog, while many people will be familiar with the chunk *rough guide* to refer to a well-known range of travel guides.

Word play and puns are the staples of English humour since so many words are polysemous or, as we have seen, are homophones or homographs (Figure 6.6). A news item that says: 'A lorry laden with glue crashed into a barrier on the M4 motorway and shed its load. Traffic was stuck there for hours' plays with the double meaning of 'stuck'. Another example is 'The physicist didn't understand how lightning worked until it struck her' (*struck* = physically hit/ suddenly see or understand something). Yet another example is 'My partner and I are in the iron and steel business; I do the ironing, my partner does the stealing'.

Figure 6.6 Millie's uncle pulled a few strings to get her a job as a puppeteer. © Jake Tebbit 2022.

Our ability to create word play can extend to phenomena such as **Spoonerisms** – where the initial sounds of pairs of words are exchanged for humorous effect. The comic film star Groucho Marx is reputed to have said *time wounds all heels*, a play on *heals all wounds*, suggesting that ageing plays havoc with one's feet. Spoonerisms are beloved of cryptic crossword setters. **Malapropisms** – the use of an inappropriate word either through ignorance of the conventional word or through a slip of the tongue can also amuse. Some which I have heard that made me smile include *kids from depraved backgrounds* (*deprived*), *semi-skilled milk* (*semi-skimmed*), *a misspelt youth* (*misspent*); for more examples, see McCarthy (2021c: 107–109).

EDUCATION AND LEARNING

GROWING UP WITH WORDS

At the beginning of Chapter 5, we noted the remarkable achievement of children's vocabulary acquisition, going from zero to thousands of words in a seemingly effortless progression. But the growth of vocabulary also involves education and schooling, which often requires quite a lot of effort. National curricula for English language typically set out how the child is supposed to build their vocabulary. The first task is to become familiar with the relationship between spoken words and written words, for written words will be of great importance in the child's journey through the educational hurdles. The National Curriculum for England states:

> Spoken language underpins the development of reading and writing. The quality and variety of language that pupils hear and speak are vital for developing their vocabulary and grammar and their understanding for reading and writing.[11]

It goes on to state:

> Skilled word reading involves both the speedy working out of the pronunciation of unfamiliar printed words (decoding) and the speedy recognition of familiar printed words. Underpinning both is the understanding that the letters on the page represent the sounds in spoken words.

Many of the concepts we have discussed in the previous chapters in this book (here in bold) are foregrounded in the curriculum documents:

> As vocabulary increases, teachers should show pupils how to understand the **relationships between words**, how to understand **nuances in meaning**, and how to develop their understanding of, and ability to use, **figurative language**. They should also teach pupils how to work out and clarify the meanings of unknown words and **words with more than 1 meaning**.

The early years in the English curriculum also stress the importance of children understanding suffixes and derived words. There is also an emphasis on the terminology needed to discuss vocabulary, including metaphor. Then by the age of around 12, the task becomes increasingly concerned with subject-specific vocabulary, which will be essential for students as they make life-choices and enter different disciplinary and professional fields.

In Australia, there is also an emphasis on the local variety; the Australian curriculum states that children should:

> Understand that Standard Australian English is one of many social dialects used in Australia, and that while it originated in England it has been influenced by many other languages.
> Understand that Standard Australian English is a living language within which the creation and loss of words and the evolution of usage is ongoing.[12]

The New Zealand National Curriculum document includes a focus on the 'ability to select precise vocabulary and idiom for the purpose and situation' (New Zealand Ministry of Education 1994: 20). Other parts of the English-speaking world have different issues to contend with. In Kenya, for example, the linguist and language planning expert Kembo-Sure has argued that the local variety of English is a useful tool for national communication alongside local languages which are on hand for more intimate social interactions. Meanwhile, the teaching of international varieties of English or English as a lingua franca has been seen to be a more specialized task, mostly of use for those engaged in certain professions (Kembo-Sure 1991). In another article, Kembo-Sure (2003) lists vocabulary differences between Kenyan English and BrE and advocates a refocus towards the cultural realities of African societies in the teaching of English.

SECOND-LANGUAGE VOCABULARY

This book is primarily about first-language (L1) English vocabulary, and much of the description of how vocabulary works in previous chapters applies to the vocabulary of English as a second or foreign language too. In Chapter 5, we looked at the monolingual, bilingual, and multilingual lexicons. However, there are differences and factors which affect the millions of people around the world who are tackling English vocabulary as a second language (L2). Not least is the challenge of focusing their learning on depth as well as breadth. **Breadth** of vocabulary knowledge refers to how many words and expressions a learner knows and can use. **Depth** refers to what they know about those items: the learner has to confront pronunciation, spelling (maybe a new alphabet too), denotation, connotation, register, collocations, chunks and idiom-proneness, and metaphorical and cultural connotations to name but some of the challenges.

The challenge of achieving depth of knowledge is related to how many encounters a learner can hope to have with a new word or expression. Little children have thousands of encounters with everyday vocabulary items in their early years and absorb new material like a sponge. Learners may hardly have more than a handful of encounters with new words, since, as we saw in Chapter 1, beyond the first couple of thousand most frequent words, most English words occur only infrequently, and many learners only ever encounter them in class and in textbooks. There is also the problem of **false friends**, words, and expressions which may look the same or similar in the learner's L1 and in English, but which have different meanings. For example, English has the adverbs *actually* and *ultimately*; Spanish has *actualmente* and *últimamente* – neither of which overlaps completely in meaning with its English counterpart. On the other hand, learners may be helped along the way by the existence of **cognates** which are words in different languages which have common ancestors: English *sister* and Swedish *syster*, Spanish *enorme* and English *enormous* are examples where speakers of one language should not have too much trouble in understanding the cognate forms in the other language.

There is also the question of congruency which we touched on briefly in relation to idioms in Chapter 4. The degree of congruency between the collocations and chunks in the L1 and the L2 will affect how L2 learners process such chunks. Congruency, frequency, and the persistent influence of the L1 may all come into play in how successfully a learner can handle L2 collocations and chunks (Wolter and Gyllstad 2013). As with every other aspect of vocabulary discussed in this book, the picture is complex, and much remains to be clarified and fully understood.

THE END OF THE BEGINNING

We have come to the end of this book. It is a book about the 'basics' and so, in a sense, it is just the beginning of what I hope will be a fascinating and endlessly rewarding intellectual quest for you. Of all the areas of study within English linguistics, few are as rich and complex as its vocabulary. It is the centre of operations for creating new forms and new meanings and is the main transmitter and receiver for sharing our human experience. It is an organism that has evolved over two millennia and which continues to evolve as the societies it serves evolve, in its original motherland of England and in its wealth of independent, flourishing varieties around the world.

FURTHER READING

Carter, R. 2012. *Vocabulary: Applied Linguistic Perspectives.* **Abingdon, Oxon: Routledge.**
Ron Carter's book gives a comprehensive coverage of our main themes relevant to both first- and second-language vocabulary. It includes sections on literary stylistics and on dictionaries and looks at how vocabulary contributes to creating internal cohesion in texts. As with all Ron Carter's works, it is written in a clear, non-jargonistic style.

Kirkpatrick, A. (ed.) 2010. *The Routledge Handbook of World Englishes.* **London: Routledge.**
Andy Kirkpatrick's book brings together chapters by scholars from around the world and takes us through English varieties and their evolution, including the English of the USA, Canada, England, Ireland, Australia, and New Zealand, as

well as Africa, South and East Asia, and the Caribbean. English as a lingua franca is also discussed, and English in social contexts such as online communication and call centres is also covered.

Schmitt, N. and McCarthy, M. J. (eds.) 1997. *Vocabulary: Description, Acquisition and Pedagogy.* **Cambridge: Cambridge University Press.**

In this book, my colleague Norbert Schmitt and I brought together a collection of articles by notable researchers in the field of second-language vocabulary studies. There are chapters on describing vocabulary, how it is acquired, and on vocabulary teaching. Although it is primarily about second-language acquisition, much of its content is relevant also to first-language vocabulary.

NOTES

1 https://www.bbc.co.uk/news/uk-england-oxfordshire-42441025.
2 https://www.cbc.ca/radio/asithappens/as-it-happens-thursday-edition-1.4991383/b-c-students-send-letters-to-oxford-telling-dictionary-to-bring-back-lost-nature-words-1.4991389.
3 https://public.oed.com/blog/the-oed-june-2021-update/#.
4 https://www.merriam-webster.com/words-at-play/the-merriam-webster-word-o-meter.
5 https://www.bbc.co.uk/bitesize/articles/ztp9g7h.
6 https://www.australiangeographic.com.au/news/2010/08/why-we-shorten-barbie-footy-and-arvo/.
7 The data come from the British Academic Written English (BAWE) corpus, which was developed at the Universities of Warwick, Reading and Oxford Brookes under the directorship of Hilary Nesi and Sheena Gardner (formerly of the Centre for Applied Linguistics, Warwick), Paul Thompson (formerly of the Department of Applied Linguistics, Reading), and Paul Wickens (School of Education, Oxford Brookes), with funding from the ESRC (RES-000-23-0800).
8 Retrieved from https://www.afar.com/magazine/electric-planes-are-coming-sooner-than-you-think?utm_source=pocket-newtab-global-en-GB.
9 *The Sunday Times Magazine* 20 March 2022: 42.
10 *The Observer Magazine*, 18 July 2021: front cover.
11 https://www.gov.uk/government/publications/national-curriculum-in-england-english-programmes-of-study/national-curriculum-in-england-english-programmes-of-stud.
12 https://www.australiancurriculum.edu.au/.

GLOSSARY OF KEY TERMS

ablaut compound
Compound of two words which vary in their vowel sounds, e.g. *flip-flop, crisscross, chit-chat*

acronym
Set of initials pronounced as a word, e.g. *PIN* (personal identification number), *NASA, UNESCO.*

antonymy
Relation of oppositeness, e.g. *high* versus *low, love* versus *hate.* Gradable antonyms can be placed on a scale, e.g. *icy, COLD, warm, HOT.* Non-gradable antonyms are absolutes, e.g. *dead* versus *alive.*

base form
The form typically chosen as the headword in a dictionary entry, e.g. SPEAK will include *speaks, speaking, spoke* and *spoken* in its definition.

blend
A combination of two words or parts of words to produce a combined meaning, e.g. *smog (smoke + fog).*

chunk
A recurring string of words which has a unified meaning or pragmatic function, e.g. *at the end of the day; as a rule.*

clang response
A response in a word-association test based on similarity of sound (e.g. *dog > frog*).

class conversion
When a word that normally belongs to one word class is used as if it belonged to another, e.g. the verb *ask* used as a noun in *a big ask*.

clipping
Shortening of a word, often to create an informal effect, e.g. *footy* = football, *journo* = journalist.

cognate
A word in one language which has a shared ancestry and similarity with a word in another language, e.g. *enorme* in Spanish and *enormous* in English.

co-hyponym
Words which are on the same level in terms of specificity of meaning and which include a more general meaning, e.g. *tulip* and *daffodil* are co-hyponyms of *flower*.

collocation
The likelihood that two words will appear in the same environment, for example, *blonde hair* is a collocation; *blonde* and *hair* collocate; *beige* and *hair* do not collocate. *Blonde hair* is a **strong** collocation; *long hair* is a **weak** collocation (*long* can collocate with a wide range of words).

componential analysis
A method of analysing the meaning of words by breaking them down into their semantic components, e.g. *puppy* has the components + *mammal* + *canine* + *young*.

compound
A closely tied combination of words with a single, unitary meaning, e.g. *car park, windscreen wiper, headphones, ready-made*.

congruency
The degree of correspondence of meaning and wording between expressions in two languages, e.g. Spanish *coger el toro por los cuernos* corresponds directly to English *take the bull by the horns*, showing a high degree of congruency.

connotation
Associations and feelings attached to a word or expression in addition to its primary meaning.

decomposition
Breaking a word down into its sematic components. See **componential analysis**.

denotation
The primary or core meaning of a word or expression.

derivation, derived word
The creation of new words (derived words) by means of adding prefixes and suffixes.

discourse marker
Word or phrase used to organise and manage speech or writing, e.g. *you know, I mean, firstly, to sum up*.

euphemism
Use of a weaker or milder vocabulary instead of words and expressions which might be too harsh or direct, e.g. *pass away* instead of *die*.

exemplar
Word or expression used to represent a whole similar class of people or things. In *pies and things like that*, *pies* are seen as exemplars of a range of pastry goods.

false friend
A word which looks similar in another language but means something different. French *actuellement* ('currently') and English *actually* ('in fact') are false friends.

function word
Words which have grammatical (functional) meanings rather than lexical (content) meanings, e.g. articles, pronouns, conjunctions. Also called **grammar words**.

headword
The form of a word given at the beginning of a dictionary entry for that word.

homograph
A word spelt the same way as another word but pronounced differently and with a different meaning, e.g. *bass* (/bæs/ rhyming with *class*) is a type of fish; *bass* (/beɪs/ rhyming with *face*) is the lowest range of musical notes.

homonymy
Similarity between words based on their spelling and/or pronunciation.

homophone
A word pronounced the same way as another but with a different meaning, e.g. *ewe* and *you*.

hyperbole
Exaggerated use of words and expressions for intensification, emphasis, humour, etc. For example, *I've got millions of cousins*.

hyponymy
Relationship of inclusion of meaning, e.g. *rose*, *violet* and *tulip* each includes the meaning of FLOWER. See **co-hyponym**.

Idiom
Expression whose meaning cannot easily be derived from the individual words that make it up, e.g. *spill the beans* and *to be rolling in it* are idiomatic expressions.

Idiom principle
An observation first made by John Sinclair that a great proportion of our use of language is made up of prefabricated chunks rather than individual words assembled one by one.

inflection
Adding endings to words to express notions such as tense, aspect and number: *arrives, arrived* and *arriving* are inflected forms of the verb *arrive*.

initialism
The use of sets of initials instead of full words, e.g. *BBC* (British Broadcasting Corporation), *CIA* (Central Intelligence Agency).

lemma
Form of a word which represents all its inflected forms. SPEAK is normally used as the lemma form of *speak(s), spoke, spoken, speaking.*

lexical gap
When a language does not have a word to express a needed meaning. English had no single word for 'an official who investigates complaints of maladministration by the government', so it borrowed the Swedish word *ombudsman* to fill the gap.

lexical set
A set of words which express the ideas covered in a lexical field. The lexical set *stroll, amble, plod, stride,* etc. occupies the lexical field of 'walking' in English.

lexical word
A word with 'content' meaning in contrast to grammar or function words. Most of the words of English are lexical words. See **function word**.

lexicography, lexicographer
Lexicography means the writing of dictionaries. The people who write them are lexicographers.

lexicon
Another, more technical word for the vocabulary of a language.

lingua franca
A language used for communication among people where none of them may have that language as their native language. For example, English is often used as a lingua franca in international business.

litotes
Figure of speech which uses a negative to express the opposite meaning, often in an ironic way, e.g. *He isn't the easiest person to get along with* suggests he was a difficult person.

loanword
Word borrowed and incorporated into a language from another language. English *kindergarten* is a loanword from German.

malapropism
Unintentional use of the wrong word through ignorance or confusion of sound and/or meaning, e.g. *semi-skilled milk* instead of *semi-skimmed*.

marked, unmarked
Words such as *goose* and *duck* are often used to cover the male and female of their species; they are unmarked (neutral terms). *Gander* and *drake* are the marked terms (explicitly marking the sex as male).

mental lexicon
A term used to describe the network of storage and processing of words and expressions in the human mind.

meronymy
A part-whole relationship of meaning between words. *Steering wheel, accelerator pedal, windscreen, headlamps*, etc. are meronyms of MOTOR VEHICLE.

metaphor
Using a word or expression to refer to something which is not its literal meaning, e.g using the human heart to refer to the centre of something: *the heart of the matter, the heart of the city.*

metonymy
Using a related word or expression to represent a larger entity as a whole, e.g. using The White House to represent the American Presidency: *George Bush ran for the White House in 1992 and lost.*

monosemous
Having just one meaning. Many scientific and technical words have a single, specific and very precise meaning.

morpheme
The smallest meaningful unit in a language. *Box* is one syllable and one morpheme. *Potato* is three syllables (*po-ta-to*) but only one morpheme.

multi-word unit
Recurrent string of more than one word which has a unitary meaning, e.g. *now and then, in a nutshell, this, that and the other.*

over-extension
Little children often over-extend the meaning of a word by applying it to something that belongs to a different class of objects, e.g. calling all different kinds of drink *juice.*

paradigmatic
Paradigmatic relationships apply to choices within families of related words, for example, we choose between *lettuce* and *cabbage* in the lexical set of VEGETABLES; something cannot be both at once.

phrasal verb
Verb consisting of a lexical verb and a particle, for example *take off, break down, crop up.*

polysemous
Having several or many meanings. Many words in English are polysemous, especially common, everyday words, e.g. *get, light, train, table.*

pragmatics
The study of meaning in context, for example, what a speaker or writer may mean by using a particular word or expression.

prefix
Form attached to the beginning of a word which changes its meaning, e.g. *pre-, un-, im-,* as in *pre-order, unlikely, impolite.*

productivity
The extent to which a morpheme generates new words. The prefix *ig-* and the suffix *-dom* are largely unproductive in modern English, while the prefix *un-* and the suffix *-ness* produce many new words.

prototype
If something is a prototype of something, it is the example that immediately comes to mind, e.g. most British people would consider a robin or blackbird to be more prototypical of a 'bird' than an albatross or an ostrich.

response token
Word or chunk used to respond immediately to what someone has just said, e.g. *right, okay, that's great, absolutely, wow!*

rhyming compound
Compound of elements which rhyme, e.g. *big-wig, ragbag, fuddy-duddy.*

root
An element or morpheme to which prefixes and suffixes may be added, e.g. the root *press* is the basis of *express, depress, repress, compression, expressive.*

semantic field
A domain or area of meaning that relates to lexical fields and their sets of related words, e.g. the semantic fields of SPORTING ACTIVITIES or TEMPERATURE.

semantic primes
Basic terms which are universally applicable and language-independent, used to label the semantic components of words in componential analysis, e.g. + ANIMATE, + HUMAN.

semantics
The study of meaning.

sense relations
Relations of meaning between words, for example, synonymy, antonymy.

stereotypes
Core members of classes of people and things: *cars, vans, lorries* and *buses* are stereotypical vehicles, even though vehicles may include *tractors, tanks, golf-buggies* and so on

suffix
Form attached to the end of a word which changes its word class, e.g. *-ment, -ation* and *-ful*, as in *enjoyment, confirmation* and *beautiful.*

superordinate
Word attached to a class of people or things whose meaning is included in its more specific co-hyponyms, e.g. *tree* is a superordinate of *oak, ash, willow, palm, pine*, etc.

syllables
Combinations of a consonant and vowel sounds which go to make up words. *Japan* has two syllables (*Ja-pan*); *Canada* has three (*Ca-na-da*).

synonymy
A relation of sameness or similarity in meaning: *angry* and *irate, end* and *finish, at the moment* and *right now* are pairs of synonyms.

syntagmatic
How words relate to one another when they combine or occur together. Collocation is a syntagmatic relation.

under-extension
Children often under-extend the meaning of a newly learnt word, for example, hesitating to use the word *doggy* to apply more widely to dogs other than the family pet.

vague expressions
Expressions such as *things like that, and stuff, or whatever*, which enable a speaker to refer to a whole class of things without having to specify or list them all.

word
Unit of meaning consisting of at least one morpheme. In writing, words are bounded by spaces.

word association
Word association tests typically ask people to say the first word that comes into their head when they hear a cue or prompt word. Such tests are used as evidence for how words are organised in people's minds.

word family
A base form and all its derived forms considered together. *Beauty, beautiful, beautifully, beautify* and *beautification* all belong to the same word family

word form
The individual form of a word as it occurs in any text. *Say, says, saying* and *said* are different word forms, even though they are all related to the verb *say*.

word recognition
Word recognition tests are used to see how quickly people can recognise whether the prompt they hear or see is a real word in that language or not.

REFERENCES

Aitchison, J. 2012. *Words in the Mind. An Introduction to the Mental Lexicon*. Fourth edition. Oxford. Wiley-Blackwell.

Ari, O. 2016. Word recognition processes in college-age students' reading comprehension achievement. *Community College Journal of Research and Practice* 40 (8): 718–723.

Ariel, M. 2002. The demise of a unique concept of literal meaning. *Journal of Pragmatics* 34: 361–402.

Balteiro, I. 2013. Blending in English charactoons. *English Studies* 94 (8): 883–907.

Barber, C., Beal, J. C. and Shaw, P. A. (2012). *The English Language: A Historical Introduction*. Second edition. Cambridge: Cambridge University Press.

Barnden, J. 2018. Broadly reflexive relationships, a special type of hyperbole, and implications for metaphor and metonymy. *Metaphor and Symbol* 33 (3): 218–234.

Bauer, L. and Renouf, A. 2001. A corpus-based study of compounding in English. *Journal of English Linguistics* 29 (2): 101–123.

Biber, D. 2009. A corpus-driven approach to formulaic language: Multi-word patterns in speech and writing. *International Journal of Corpus Linguistics* 14: 381–417.

Blake, N. 2004. *Shakespeare's Non-standard English: A dictionary of His Informal Language*. London: Continuum.

Boberg, C. 2005. The North American regional vocabulary survey: New variables and methods in the study of North American English. *American Speech* 80 (1): 22–60.

Boers, F. and Stengers, H. 2008. A quantitative comparison of the English and Spanish repertoires of figurative idioms. In F. Boers and S. Lindstromberg (eds.), *Cognitive Linguistic Approaches to Teaching Vocabulary and Phraseology*. Berlin, New York: De Gruyter Mouton, 355–374.

Bohmann, A. 2019. *Variation in English Worldwide: Registers and Global Varieties*. Cambridge: Cambridge University Press.

Bolinger, D. L. 1963. It's so fun. *American Speech* 38 (3): 236–240.

Bolinger, D. L. 1965. The atomization of meaning. *Language* 41 (4): 555–573.

Brezina, V., Gablasova, D. and Reichelt, S. 2018. *BNClab*. Retrieved from http://corpora.lancs.ac.uk/bnclab [electronic resource], Lancaster University.

Brown, R. 1958. How shall a thing be called? *Psychological Review* 65 (1): 14–21.

Bruza, P., Kitto, K., Nelson, D. and McEvoy, C. 2009. Is there something quantum-like about the human mental lexicon? *Journal of Mathematical Psychology* 53: 362–377.

Buchanan, D. C. 1965. *Japanese Proverbs and Sayings, Volume 1*. Norman: University of Oklahoma Press.

Buchanan, L and Westbury, C. 2001. Characterizing semantic space: Neighborhood effects in word recognition. *Psychonomic Bulletin & Review* 8 (3): 531–544.

Burnley, D. 1992. Lexis and semantics. In N. Blake (ed.), *The Cambridge History of the English Language*. Cambridge: Cambridge University Press, 409–499.

Buttery, P. and McCarthy, M. J. In press. Lexis in spoken discourse. In J. Gee and M. Handford (eds.), *The Routledge Handbook of Discourse Analysis*. Second Edition. Abingdon, Oxon: Routledge.

Cacciari, C. and Glucksberg, S. 1995. Understanding idioms: Do visual images reflect figurative meanings? *European Journal of Cognitive Psychology* 7 (3): 283–305.

Cambridge 1997. *Cambridge International Dictionary of Phrasal Verbs*. Cambridge: Cambridge University Press.

Cannon, G. 1986. Blends in English word formation. *Linguistics* 24 (4): 725–754.

Carroll, L. 1872/1998. *Alice's Adventures in Wonderland and Through the Looking Glass*. Centenary Edition. London: Penguin Books.

Carter, R. and McCarthy, M. J. 1997. *Exploring Spoken English*. Cambridge: Cambridge University Press.

Carter, R. and McCarthy, M. J. 2006. *Cambridge Grammar of English*. Cambridge: Cambridge University Press.

Cawdrey, R. 1604/1966. *Table Alphabeticall of Hard Usual English Words*. Gainesville, Florida: Scholars' Facsimiles & Reprints.

Chabot, R. J., Zehr, H. D., Prinzo, O. V. and Petros, T. V. 1984. The speed of word recognition subprocesses and reading achievement in college students. *Reading Research Quarterly* 19 (2): 147–161.

Cheshire, J. (ed.) 1991. *English around the World: Sociolinguistic Perspectives.* Cambridge: Cambridge University Press.

Chomsky, N. 1959. Review of *Verbal Behavior* by B. F. Skinner. *Language* 35 (1): 26–58.

Chovanec, J. 2019. Euphemisms and non-proximal manipulation of discourse space: The case of *blue-on-blue. Lingua* 225: 50–62.

Coghill, N. 2003. *The Canterbury Tales.* Introduction by Nevill Coghill. Penguin Classics edition. London: Penguin Books Ltd.

Colston, H. L. 1997. "I've Never Seen Anything Like It": Overstatement, understatement, and irony. *Metaphor and Symbol* 12 (1): 43–58.

Colston, H. L. and O'Brien, J. 2000a. Contrast of kind versus contrast of magnitude: The pragmatic accomplishments of irony and hyperbole. *Discourse Processes* 30 (2): 179–199.

Colston, H. L. and O'Brien, J. 2000b. Contrast and pragmatics in figurative language: Anything understatement can do, irony can do better. *Journal of Pragmatics* 32: 1557–1583.

Cook, G. 2001. *The Discourse of Advertising.* Second edition. London: Routledge.

Corpas Pastor, G. 2021. Constructional idioms of 'insanity' in English and Spanish: A corpus-based study. *Lingua* 254: 1–20.

Cronk, B. C. and Schweigert, W. A. 1992. The comprehension of idioms: The effects of familiarity, literalness, and usage. *Applied Psycholinguists* 13: 131–146.

Cruse, D. A. 1975. *Lexical Semantics.* Cambridge: Cambridge University Press.

Cruse, D. A. 1977. The pragmatics of lexical specificity. *Journal of Linguistics* 13 (2): 153–164.

Crystal, D. 2005. *The Stories of English.* London: Penguin Books.

Crystal, D. 2010. *Begat: The King James Bible and the English Language.* Oxford: Oxford University Press.

Cutler, A. 1981. The reliability of speech error data. *Linguistics* 19: 561–582.

Cutting, J. (ed.) 2007. *Vague Language Explored.* Basingstoke, Hants: Palgrave Macmillan.

Deignan, A. 2005a. A corpus linguistic perspective on the relationship between metonymy and metaphor. *Style* 1: 72–91.

Deignan, A. 2005b. *Metaphor and Corpus Linguistics.* Amsterdam: John Benjamins.

Denison, D., and Hogg, R. 2006. Overview. In R. Hogg and D. Denison (eds), *A History of the English Language.* Cambridge: Cambridge University Press, 1–42.

De Ruiter, L. and Theakston, A. 2017. First language acquisition. In B. Dancygier (ed.), *The Cambridge Handbook of Cognitive Linguistics.* Cambridge: Cambridge University Press, 59–72.

Dong, Y., Gui, S. and MacWhinney, B. 2005. Shared and separate meanings in the bilingual mental lexicon. *Bilingualism: Language and Cognition* 8 (3): 221–238.

Elman, J. E. 2004. An alternative view of the mental lexicon. *Trends in Cognitive Sciences* 8 (7): 301–306.

Emmorey, K., and Fromkin, V. 1988. The mental lexicon. In F. Newmeyer (ed.), *Linguistics: The Cambridge Survey*. Cambridge: Cambridge University Press, 124–149.

Erman, B. and Warren, B. 2000. The idiom principle and the open choice principle. *Text and Talk* 20 (1): 29–62.

Ervin, S. M. 1961. Changes with age in the verbal determinants of word-association. *The American Journal of Psychology* 74 (3): 361–372.

Farr, F. and Murphy, B. 2009. Religious references in contemporary Irish English: 'For the love of God almighty.... I'm a holy terror for turf'. *Intercultural Pragmatics* 6 (4): 535–555.

Ferber, R. 1995. Reliability and validity of slip-of-the-tongue corpora: A methodological note. *Linguistics* 33: 1169–1190.

Firth, J. R. 1951/1957. *Papers in Linguistics*. Oxford: Oxford University Press, 190–215.

Fitzpatrick, T., Playfoot, D., Wray, A. and Wright, M. J. 2015. Establishing the reliability of word association data for investigating individual and group differences. *Applied Linguistics* 36 (1): 23–50.

Fitzpatrick, T. and Thwaites, P. 2020. Word association research and the L2 lexicon. *Language Teaching* 53: 237–274.

Fox Tree, J. E. and Schrock, J. C. 2002. Basic meanings of *you know* and *I mean*. *Journal of Pragmatics* 34: 727–747.

Gagné, C. L., Spalding, T. L. and Schmidtke, D. 2019. LADEC: The large database of English compounds. *Behavior Research Methods* 51: 2152–2179.

Gibbs, R. W. 1980. Spilling the beans on understanding and memory for idioms in conversation. *Memory & Cognition* 8 (2): 149–156.

Gibbs, R. W. 1986. Skating on thin ice: Literal meaning and understanding idioms in conversation *Discourse Processes* 9 (1): 17–30.

Gibbs, R. W. 1992. What do idioms really mean? *Journal of Memory and Language* 31: 485–506.

Gibbs Jr., R. W., Colston, H. L. and Johnson, M. D. 1996. Proverbs and the metaphorical mind. *Metaphor and Symbol* 11 (3): 207–216.

Giora, R. 1999. On the priority of salient meanings: Studies of literal and figurative language. *Journal of Pragmatics* 31: 919–929.

Gooden, P. 2011. *The Story of English: How the English Language Conquered the World*. London: Quercus.

Grice, P. 1975. Logic and conversation. In P. Cole and J. Morgan (eds.), *Syntax and Semantics. 3: Speech Acts*. New York: Academic Press, 41–58.

Guerrero, L., Clareta, A., Verbeke, W., Enderli, G., Zakowska-Biemans, S., Vanhonacker, F., Issanchou, S., Sajdakowska, M., Granli, B. S., Scalvedi, L., Contel, M. and Hersleth, M. 2010. Perception of traditional food products in six European regions using free word association. *Food Quality and Preference* 21 (2): 225–233.

Guy, G. R. 1991. Australia. In J. Cheshire (ed.), *English around the World: Sociolinguistic Perspectives*. Cambridge: Cambridge University Press, 213–226.

Halliday, M. A. K. 1975. *Learning How to Mean: Explorations in the Development of Language*. London: Edward Arnold.

Hashim, A. and Leitner, G. 2011. Contact expressions in contemporary Malaysian English. *World Englishes* 30 (4): 551–568.

Hogg, R. 2006. English in Britain. In R. Hogg and D. Denison (eds.), *A History of the English Language*. Cambridge: Cambridge University Press, 352–383.

Hübler, A. 1983. *Understatements and Hedges in English*. Amsterdam: John Benjamins.

Hughes, A. and Trudgill, P. 1979. *English Accents and Dialects*. London: Edward Arnold.

Huler, S. 2018. What's a dictionary's job? To tell us how to use words or to show us how we're using them? The Washington Post. Retrieved 01 March 2022 from https://www.washingtonpost.com/entertainment/books/kids-dont-know-what-nature-means--but-thats-not-the-dictionarys-problem/2018/01/25/8df5c866-fbcc-11e7-a46b-a3614530bd87_story.html.

Kastovsky, D. 2006. Vocabulary. In R. Hogg and D. Denison (eds.), *A History of the English Language*. Cambridge: Cambridge University Press, 199–270.

Katz, J. J. and Fodor, J. A. 1963. The structure of a semantic theory. *Language* 39 (2): 170–210.

Kembo-Sure 1991. Learning English in Kenya: Problems and causes. *Language, Culture and Curriculum* 4 (2): 133–138.

Kembo-Sure 2003. Establishing a national standard and English language curriculum change in Kenya. *Language Culture and Curriculum* 16 (2): 197–211.

Knowles, G. 1997. *A Cultural History of the English Language*. London: Arnold.

Kreuz, R. J. and Roberts, R. M. 1995. Two cues for verbal irony: Hyperbole and the ironic tone of voice. *Metaphor and Symbol* 10 (1): 21–31.

Lakoff, G. and Johnson, M. 1980/2003. *Metaphors We Live By*. 2003 edition. Chicago, IL: The University of Chicago Press.

Layton, J. R. 1979. Hyperbole, metaphor and simile, words not to be taken too literally: Animal, vegetable, and mineral. *Language Arts* 56 (7): 778–783.

Lehrer, A. 1969. Semantic cuisine. *Journal of Linguistics* 5 (1): 39–55.

Lehrer, A. 2012. A theory of meaning. *Philosophical Studies: An International Journal for Philosophy in the Analytic Tradition* 161 (1): 97–107.

Lehrer, A. and Kittay, E. F. (eds) 1992/2009. *Frames, Fields, and Contrasts: New Essays in Semantic and Lexical Organization*. Abingdon, Oxon: Routledge.

Libben, G. 2000. Representation and processing in the second language lexicon: The homogeneity hypothesis. In J. Archibald (ed.), *Second Language Acquisition and Linguistic Theory*. Oxford: Blackwell, 228–248.

Littlemore, J. 2015. *Metonymy: Hidden Shortcuts in Language, Thought and Communication*. Cambridge: Cambridge University Press.

Locke, J. 1986. Speech perception and the emergent lexicon: An ethological approach. In P. Fletcher and M. Garman (eds.), *Language Acquisition: Studies in First Language Development*. Cambridge: Cambridge University Press, 240–250.

Love, R., Dembry, C., Hardie, A., Brezina, V. and McEnery, T. 2017. The spoken BNC2014: Designing and building a spoken corpus of everyday conversations. *International Journal of Corpus Linguistics* 22 (3): 319–344.

Lyons, J. 1977. *Semantics. Volume 1*. Cambridge: Cambridge University Press.

Lyons, J. 1995. *Linguistic Semantics*. Cambridge: Cambridge University Press.

Machan, T. W. 1994. Language contact in *Piers Plowman*. *Speculum* 69 (2): 359–385.

Martin, T. P. 1986. Joyce and Wagner's Pale Vampire. *James Joyce Quarterly* 23 (4): 491–496.

Martinez, R. and Schmitt, N. 2012. A phrasal expressions list. *Applied Linguistics* 33 (3): 299–320.

McCarthy, M. J. 1998. *Spoken Language and Applied Linguistics*. Cambridge: Cambridge University Press.

McCarthy, M. J. 2002. Good listenership made plain: British and American non-minimal response tokens in everyday conversation. In R. Reppen, S. Fitzmaurice and D. Biber (eds.), *Using Corpora to Explore Linguistic Variation*. Amsterdam: John Benjamins, 49–71.

McCarthy, M. J. 2003. Talking back: 'Small' interactional response tokens in everyday conversation. *Research on Language in Social Interaction* 36 (1): 33–63.

McCarthy, M. J. 2021a. *Innovations and Challenges in Grammar*. Abingdon, Oxon: Routledge.

McCarthy, M. J. 2021b. *English Grammar: The Basics*. Abingdon, Oxon: Routledge.

McCarthy, M. J. 2021c. *McCarthy's Field Guide to Grammar: Natural English Usage and Style*. London: Chambers.

McCarthy, M. J. and Carter, R. 2004. "There's millions of them": hyperbole in everyday conversation. *Journal of Pragmatics* 36: 149–184.

McGlone, M. S., Beck, G. and Pfiester, A. 2006. Contamination and camouflage in euphemisms. *Communication Monographs* 73 (3): 261–282.

Milroy, J. 2007. The history of English. In D. Britain (ed.), *Language in the British Isles*. Cambridge: Cambridge University Press, 9–33.

Moon, R. 1998. *Fixed Expressions and Idioms in English*. Oxford: Clarendon Press.

Morwood, J. and Warman, M. 2008. *Our Greek and Latin Roots*. Second edition. Cambridge: Cambridge University Press.

Murphy, M. L. 2003. *Semantic Relations and the Lexicon: Antonymy, Synonymy and Other Paradigms*. Cambridge: Cambridge University Press.

Murphy, M. L. 2010. *Lexical Meaning*. Cambridge: Cambridge University Press.

Nation, I. S. P. and Coxhead, A. 2021. *Measuring Native-Speaker Vocabulary Size*. Amsterdam: John Benjamins.

Nevalainen, T. and Van Ostade, I. 2006. Standardisation. In R. Hogg and D. Denison (eds.), *A History of the English Language*. Cambridge: Cambridge University Press, 271–311.

New Zealand Ministry of Education 1994. *English in the New Zealand Curriculum*. Wellington: Learning Media Ltd.

Niemi, J., Mulli, J., Nenonen, M., Niemi, S., Nikolaev, A. and Penttilä, E. 2013. Idiomatic proclivity and literality of meaning in body-part nouns: Corpus studies of English, German, Swedish, Russian and Finnish. *Folia Linguistica* 47 (1): 237–252.

O'Keeffe, A. and Adolphs, S. 2008. Response tokens in British and Irish English. In K. P. Schneider and A. Barron (eds.), *Variational Pragmatics*. Amsterdam: John Benjamins, 69–98.

Oppenheimer, S. 2006. *The Origins of the British: A Genetic Detective Story*. London: Constable.

Piirainen, E. 2005. Europeanism, internationalism or something else? Proposal for a cross-lingustic and cross-cultural research project on widespread idioms in Europe and beyond. *HERMES - Journal of Language and Communication in Business* 18 (35): 45–75.

Piirainen, E. 2010. The convergence of European idioms and the so-called globalization. In A. P. ten Cate, R. Rapp, J. Strässler, M. Vliegen and H. Weber (eds.), *Grammatik. Praxis. Geschichte. Festschrift für Wilfried Kürschner*. Tübingen: Narr, 343–350.

Pillai, S. and Ong, L. T. 2018. English(es) in Malaysia. *Asian Englishes* 20 (2): 147–157.

Ritchie, D. L. 2013. *Metaphor*. Cambridge: Cambridge University Press.

Rodríguez-Puente, P. 2019. *The English Phrasal Verb, 1650-Present*. Cambridge: Cambridge University Press.

Rosch, E. 1973. Natural categories. *Cognitive Psychology* 4: 328–350.

Rosch, E. and Mervis, C. B. 1975. Family resemblances: Studies in the internal structure of categories. *Cognitive Psychology* 7: 573–605.

Rosch, E., Mervis, C. B., Gray, Johnson, D. M. and Boyes-Braem, P. 1976. Basic objects in natural categories. *Cognitive Psychology* 8: 382–439.

Rosenzweig, M. R. 1961. Comparisons among word-association responses in English, French, German, and Italian. *The American Journal of Psychology* 74 (3): 347–360.

Rothman, J., Amaro, J. and De Bot, K. 2013. Third language acquisition. In J. Herschensohn and M. Young-Scholten (eds.), *The Cambridge Handbook of Second Language Acquisition*. Cambridge: Cambridge University Press, 372–393.

Rubio-Fernández, P., Wearing, C. and Carston, R. 2015. Metaphor and hyperbole: Testing the continuity hypothesis. *Metaphor and Symbol* 30 (1): 24–40.

Sanchez-Stockhammer, C. 2018. *English Compounds and Their Spelling*. Cambridge: Cambridge University Press.

Schmitt, N. (ed.) 2004. *Formulaic Sequences*. Amsterdam: John Benjamins.

Schneider, E. W. 2009. English in North America. In B. B. Kachru, Y. Kachru and C. L. Nelson. (eds.), *The Handbook of World Englishes*. Oxford: Wiley Blackwell, 58–73.

Silva-Corvalán, C. 2014. *Bilingual Language Acquisition: Spanish and English in the First Six Years*. Cambridge: Cambridge University Press.

Sinclair, J. McH. 1987. *Collins COBUILD English Language Dictionary*. London: Collins.

Sinclair, J. McH. 1991. *Corpus, Concordance, Collocation*. Oxford: Oxford University Press.

Singleton, D. 2016. *Language and the Lexicon: An Introduction*. Abingdon, Oxon: Routledge.

Snow, C. 1986. Conversations with children. In P. Fletcher and M. Garman (eds.), *Language Acquisition: Studies in First Language Development*. Cambridge: Cambridge University Press, 69–89.

Spőttl, C. and McCarthy, M. J. 2003. Formulaic utterances in the multi-lingual context. In J. Cenoz, U. Jessner and B. Hufeisen (eds.), *The Multilingual Lexicon*. Dordrecht: Kluwer, 133–151.

Spőttl, C. and McCarthy, M. J. 2004. Comparing the knowledge of formulaic sequences across L1, L2, L3 and L4. In N. Schmitt (ed.), *Formulaic Sequences*. Amsterdam: John Benjamins, 191–225.

Stavans, A. and Hoffmann, C. 2015. *Multilingualism*. Cambridge: Cambridge University Press.

Stone, J. R. 2006. *The Routledge Book of World Proverbs*. London: Routledge.

Summey, G. 1951. Review of *The Compounding and Hyphenation of English Words*, by Alice Morton Ball. *The English Journal* 40 (8): 478–480.

Swanton, M. 1971. *An Anglo-Saxon Chronicle*. Exeter: University of Exeter Press.

Tent, J. 2001. A profile of the Fiji English lexis. *English World-Wide* 22 (2): 211–247.

Tent, J. and Clark, J. E. 1980. An experimental investigation into the perception of slips of the tongue. *Journal of Phonetics* 8: 317–325.

Trampe, W. 2018. Euphemisms for killing animals and for other forms of their use. In Fill, A. F. and Penz, H. (eds.), *The Routledge Handbook of Ecolinguistics*. Abingdon, Oxon: Routledge, 325–341.

Turvey, M. T. and Moreno, M. A. 2006. Physical metaphors for the mental lexicon. *The Mental Lexicon* 1 (1): 7–33.

Ullmann, S. 1962. *Semantics: An Introduction to the Science of Meaning*. Oxford: Basil Blackwell.

Umar, A. M. 2019. The structure of idioms in Nigerian English: The effects indigenous Nigerian languages have had on English idioms in Nigeria. *English Today* 35 (3): 29–34.

Walsh, S., O'Keeffe, A. and McCarthy, M. J. 2008. '… post-colonialism, multi-culturalism, structuralism, feminism, post-modernism and so on and so forth': A comparative analysis of vague category markers in academic discourse. In A. Ädel and R. Reppen (eds.), *Corpora and Discourse*. Amsterdam: John Benjamins, 9–29.

Wang, S-P. 2005. Corpus-based approaches and discourse analysis in relation to reduplication and repetition. *Journal of Pragmatics* 37: 505–540.

Warren-Leubecker, A. and Bohannon, J. N. 1984. Intonation patterns in child-directed speech: Mother-father speech. *Child Development* 55 (4): 1379–1385.

Wierzbicka, A. 1986. Does language reflect culture? Evidence from Australian English. *Language in Society* 15 (3): 349–373.

Wilson, C. 2022. Strawberry yields forever. *New Scientist Magazine*, 5 March 2022: 51.

Wolter, B. and Gyllstad, H. 2013. Frequency of input and L2 collocational processing: A comparison of congruent and incongruent collocations. *Studies in Second Language Acquisition* 35 (3): 451–482.

Womak, J. 2020. *Homunculus*. Manchester: Carcanet.

Wong, M. 2017. *Hong Kong English. Exploring Lexicogrammar and Discourse from a Corpus Linguistic Perspective*. Basingstoke Hants: Palgrave Macmillan.

Wood, M. 2005. *In Search of the Dark Ages*. London: BBC Books.

Wray, A. 2000. Formulaic sequences in second language teaching: Principle and practice. *Applied Linguistics* 21: 463–489.

Wray, A. 2002. *Formulaic Language and the Lexicon*. Cambridge: Cambridge University Press.

INDEX

*Cambridge International Dictionary of
    Phrasal Verbs* 13
Cambridgeshire 148
Cameroon 147
Canada 3, 132, 145
Cannon, G. 20
Canterbury Tales 38, 40, 42
Cantonese 145
caretaker speech 109
Caribbean 3, 50
Carroll, L. 6, 20
Carter, R. 15, 99, 108, 159
Cawdrey, R. 43, 131
Caxton, W. 38, 40
Celtic 30, 31
Chabot, R. J. 121
Chaucer, G. 38, 40, 42
Cheshire, J. 147
child directed speech (CDS) 109–10
Childes English Corpus 111
Chomsky, N. 107–8
Chovanec, J. 103
chunks 14–15, 81–5, 127–8, 144, 150
clang responses 123
Clark, E. V. 129
Clark, J. E. 125
class conversion 12
clipping 21
clusters 15, 81
Cockney 3, 148
Coghill, N. 39
cognates 158
co-hyponyms 64, 67–9, 137, 153
collocation 17, 124, 134
colour terms 122, 141
Colston, H. L. 100–2
co-meronyms 68–9
complementaries 62
complete synonymy 59
componential analysis 71–5
compounds 10–13
conceptual metaphors 92–4
concordances 26, 28
congruency 91, 159
connotation 56, 153

consonant clusters 111
converse antonyms 63
cooing 108
Cook, G. 153
Cornish 30
Corpas Pastor, G. 91
corpora 23–8, 133–4
Coxhead, A. 106
Cronk, B. C. 85
Cruse, D. A. 69–71, 77
Crystal, D. 36, 47, 51
Cutting, J. 138
Cyprus 4

Danelaw 35
Danish 35
De Ruiter, L. 112
decomposition 71, 81
Deignan, A. 98, 99, 105
Denison, D. 35
denotation 54, 56, 59, 79
depth of vocabulary knowledge 158
derivation 8, 19
descriptive 133
dialects 3, 33, 35, 38, 51, 147–9
dictionaries 11, 19, 43, 131–3
discourse markers 26, 139
Dong, Y. 127

Elizabeth I 45
Elman, J. E. 118
emergent meaning 136
Emmorey, K. 118
encyclopaedic knowledge 54, 85
entailment 66
Erman, B. 15
Ervin, S. M. 122–3
Eswatin 147
euphemisms 103
exemplars 137

false friends 158
Farr, F. 144
Ferber, R. 125
figurative meaning 78–9